Encountering Life's Endings

Encountering Life's Endings

Louis Silverstein

To order additional copies of this book, contact:
Xlibris Corporation
1-888-795-4274
www.Xlibris.com
Orders@Xlibris.com
57414

Contents

For all those who have shared their lives with me,
especially Jack, Yetta, Al, Joe and Eddie.
Know that you live on in my heart always.
The journey continues.

Prologue

Summer 2007

ORKING ON MY sabbatical project—writing a book on the subject of death and dying. I could not have imagined what fate had in store for me as words and images on paper would once again be swamped by a tsunami of reality in the form of my heart being pierced by the loss of a loved one.

Nine thousand feet up with two thousand more to go in order to reach the summit of Haleakala, The House of the Sun, a dormant volcano on the island of Maui. Sitting across from me in the passenger seat is Al, my older brother, the patriarch of the family since our father's passing. He takes up much less room now that his entire self fits into a small plastic bag, the cremated remains of a man who once was 5'11" tall and weighed one hundred and forty-five pounds.

Save for an early morning walk along a sun-drenched beach, followed by a swim in an ocean smooth as glass, this is how my summer vacation is ending. A scattering of my brother's ashes into an earth edifice millions of years old, where he will join his father, mother and two younger brothers, they, too, traveling in the eternal represented by Haleakala.

Now, ashes in hand, eyes filled with tears, breathing deeply, I stand on the rim of the volcano, reminding Al that he is returning home, body no longer encapsulated in matter, where his beloved family awaits with open and loving arms to guide him on his next journey. His ashes are cast into the crater, as if they were a ship leaving port, but never to return home again. I see a vision of Al before me. "Till we meet again," I say to myself as much as to him.

Six weeks ago, as our plane flew low over the waters surrounding Maui, about to land on the runway of an airport I know so well, this being my twentieth visit to the Pacific paradise, I wondered what summer 2007 would have in store for me. Heaven, I knew, was waiting for me, but hell?

The hell of knowing that all life, including our loved ones as well as ourselves, will grow old and die.

The hell of being witness to the suffering my brother endured as he struggled with cancer, mirroring the struggles my other brothers went through during their journeys into the realm of terminal illness.

The hell of being the last surviving member of my birth family, separated from my father's concoction of milk and Pepsi Cola; my mother's famous chicken soup spiked with sugar; my brother Joe's smile that lit up every room he entered; my brother Edward being my traveling companion into multiple realms of consciousness; and Al's big brother advice.

The hell of loved ones I had grown accustomed to having in my life now on the other side, separated by a barrier only to be breached by my passing.

The heaven of stilling the chattering monkey in my mind while sitting on a moss covered boulder in the west Maui mountains being fully present with neither past nor future taking me away from being in the present moment.

The heaven of journeys into consciousness that open doors of perception into the realization that reality is fluid, not fixed, and that at every moment in time, we choose, knowingly or unknowingly, what to make of our lives.

The heaven of Paula, my wife of twenty-eight years, and I reconnecting as soul mates, reminding us that a successful marriage is a multi-act play with a very long run, calling for ventures into deep caverns and turbulent as well as challenging emotional seas. Explorations of marriages necessary to keep what once was a vibrant tropical forest of wedded life from experiencing relationship cooling, turning it into an arid desert.

The heaven of walking hand in hand on the beach with Paula watching marvelous sunsets, eyes feasting on sky canvases painted with such vibrant colors as to stagger the imagination.

The heaven of walking slowly, very slowly, into Garden of Eden forests, taking in each miracle that nature, our preferred house of worship, offers unto us.

The heaven of realizing, after once again having to bear the loss of a family member, that wherever I am, be it on an island nestled in the warmth of the blue Pacific, or in a small Midwestern city covered with snow, if I am with those I love, I am in paradise.

The heaven of dancing amidst other sultry bodies in heat to the beat of music that awakens the body to the sensual pleasures residing within it, yearning to be called upon to celebrate the blessing of being embodied.

The heaven of making passionate and beautiful love with the women of my dreams as body is transformed into temple and sex becomes prayer. Afterwards, drifting off into asleep in each other's arms, knowing we will be together till death do us part, be it this very moment or years from now.

The heaven in the form of witnessing rainbows arching through the sky of such breadth and depth shining on the earth as if to transform it into a work of art fit for habitation by souls of a higher nature, causing one to wonder why making peace, justice, beauty and joy are not at the core of why we are here?

My plane is about to land at Chicago's O'Hare airport.

It is good to be alive.

Introduction

You grieve for those that should not be grieved for.
The wise grieve neither for the living nor the dead.
Never at any time was I not.
Nor thou, nor these princes of men.
Nor will we cease to be hereafter.
For the unreal has no being and the real never ceases
        to be.

Bhagavad-Gita

Summer 2008

AS I STAND on a cliff on the north shore of Kauai viewing the setting of the sun, my thoughts turn to how our lives are reflective of the nature of this star sailing across the universe. Sky ablaze with the colors of red, blue orange, pink and yellow, changing ever so slowly into a steel gray and vibrant black filled canvass amidst a pervasive stillness.

At our essence we are stardust, children of the sun. Is it not to be expected that the rhythm or our lives reflect the eternal cycle of sunrise and sunset? We are born, ascend to shine brightly, descend as the light within us fades, and depart this life, returning to being dust. Left behind are memories of a life once so present in the eyes of we who are graced to behold the miracle of existence and non-existence at play in the world.

Universal and timeless, indifferent to boundaries of age, culture, race, religion or spiritual practice, ethnicity, gender, wealth, status, education, and geography, all that which divides us from one another, dying and death are life journeys central to the human experience. All that lives is fragile and impermanent and will cease to exist. No matter how much money, time, or effort is lavished on bodies, regardless of how much they are exercised, pampered or monitored, bodies die. This reality is the collective destiny of humankind.

Heads stooped with sorrow, eyes filled with tears, hands reaching out but coming up empty, hearts overflowing with sorrow, thoughts and feelings wrestling with the mourning coursing through our bodies as the ties that bind us to our loved ones become unraveled, the pain, grief and anguish of loss and separation, of silence and desolation, are overpowering and vast, and seem greater than we can endure.

We are sorely tested when we are faced with a loved ones ordeal we cannot fix. Hearts are broken when we realize that our wish to shield those we love from pain and fear is beyond our grasp as we are called upon to bear witness to the unbearable— to see a loved one suffer, be it while alive or dying.

During such times, it is helpful if we can imagine ourselves as a branch of a tree, able to sway amidst life's trials and tribulations without being broken. Although we cannot always find or construct a solution for the pain being endured by those we love, we can stay connected by being fully present and listen with compassionate hearts to their needs and desires.

We possess a deep wish that human bonds forged during our lives will transcend the severing we experience and endure at the time of death. Can a wish of this nature become a reality? The answer will be known at the end of our lives. Yet faith in the boundless potential of the human spirit to fashion a deeper meaning amidst life's challenges and crises joined to love of a nature and depth transcending time and space, and an abiding conviction in knowing that those who have crossed over still live on in our hearts and minds for divine essence never dies, can serve to bring acceptance, tranquility and peace to our troubled souls.

My Family

Dying is at its heart a sacred act. It is itself a time, a space and a process of surrender and transformation. Within the suffering that arises with loss or dying there are also the seeds of grace. These transitions are often uncomfortable, challenging old patterns and leaving us feeling uncertain, with a heightened sense of vulnerability. At the same time these experiences provide an extraordinary opportunity for growth, true freedom, and the exchange of love and compassion.

The willingness to open to the 10,000 joys and sorrows is a profound possibility that blossoms from spiritual practice and grace. Our difficulties can be transformed into a source of compassion, wisdom and grace. Facing certain inevitable sorrows is part of being human. Understandably, some people attempt to avoid life's pain, while others allow their heart to be broken

open and discover there a boundless healing reservoir
of compassion and love.

Frank Ostaseski, Founder, *The Metta Institute*

"LOUIS, MY SON, I have some news for you. Your father is dead. He didn't suffer." (Died at the age of 89.)

"Lou, I (brother Joe) have lung cancer and I'm going to die."

"Mom, I have something to tell you that you need to know. Joe died this morning." (Died at the age of 47.)

"Louis, I've (brother Eddie), been diagnosed with amlyodosis, one of the world's rarest diseases. There is no cure for it. I was told I have between one-half year to two years at the most to live."

"Mom, I can't believe I have to say this to you again. Eddie died this afternoon." (Died at the age of 44.)

"Lou, Hi, this is Al. Mom died this afternoon." (Died the age of 94)

"Lou, I (brother Al) have lung cancer and I don't know how long I have to live. It looks like you are going to be the last of the Silverstein family."

"Lou, Hi, this is Barbara (Al's widow). Al died this morning. He had a series of strokes, and then passed away in his sleep." (Died at the age of 69.)

Once, we were a vital and vibrant family of six, life's passions flowing through our bodies filled with the energy of the sun star that is our common place of origin. However, only I live on, the last of the Silverstein family, as moon energy entered the lives of my father, mother, and brothers, taking them on a journey through the darkness into the light. Now that almost seventy years of my journey have gone by, the wheel of life has turned almost full circle and memories of my loved ones fill my life rather than their voices. With outstretched hands, I touch their ashes, not their bodies.

Having to face and coming to know dying and death so intimately has served to make me poignantly aware of my own mortality. Neither curtains nor deceptions, irrespective of number or nature, can keep me from having to face the temporality of my existence. Yes, the bell will also toll for me. When, I cannot know, and the moment is largely out of my control, but my time to leave is coming. Such a reality can be overwhelming, driving one to drink or other forms of escapism in order to forget; or into the arms of young women, emulating the emperors of old who slept with youthful virgins believing that their life juices, vital energy neither adulterated nor diluted by life's challenges and ordeals, would seep into their bodies as a result of the exchange of fluids taking place during sexual intercourse.

However, I've never liked alcohol all that much, save for a glass of wine now and then, and I love my wife dearly, her mature and well-known body being much more of a desirable home for me than that of a stranger in the night. What kind of fool would I be were I to betray her love for and devotion to me in order to pursue yet another version of the chimera known as the fountain of youth? We have a marriage that has ripened and grown deeper as the years have gone by, its roots and branches entwined around the two of us in such a manner that to sever them would cut off my life force.

This is not the first time Paula and I have been lovers and I know it is our destiny to meet again. To return into each other's arms based on what we built together in the past, rather than on what I threw away in a frantic and fearful effort to flee from the unavoidable, is certainly worth dying for as much as it is worth living for.

Let us relish and enjoy what we have while we can, but a life oriented toward keeping what we have, be it bling or body, is futile. What we possess in the material world is transient, including our loved ones as our very own self.

Does this mean living in a state of constant anxiety and anticipation of dying that we should retire from life, fixated on the past and angst-ridden about what the future may have in store for us? Are we never to embark from the shore fearing we might not be able to cope with what may come our way or where we will go by virtue of casting off into the flow of life? Yes, if we wish to be among the living dead. No, if we wish to avail ourselves of the opportunity to take up the challenge of accepting and incorporating into living the life still to unfold before us, centered on the fullest possible experience of the gift of the present moment, the treasure of knowing it might be our last.

When death is near amidst awareness that our fate is shared by all conscious and feeling beings, often we experience a heartrending sense of the fragility and preciousness of life's moments and of life itself. From such awareness we are afforded the gift of cultivating boundless compassion for all mortals.

Yet, as my dear departed friend and colleague Brother Wayne Teasdale, a Catholic monk who walked in the world, reminded all who were blessed by his teachings, compassion is a verb as well as a noun. It is not just a warm heart and feeling sympathy, or caring for those who suffer and in pain due to life's misfortunes, but a life practice to reach out to and commit oneself to lessen the suffering of others.

To say what needs to be expressed and to do what needs to done from this point on so that our lives may come to an end in peace is the gift of allowing ourselves to accept in the deepest part of body, mind and soul the realization, as is the case in all that life consists of, the good and the bad, achievements and disappointments, joys and the sorrows, pleasures and pains, even life itself, will pass. Always remember that tomorrow is a possibility, not a certainty. Promises premised on the coming of a tomorrow cannot always be kept. So get on with life. Be the bearer of gifts to all who are alive. The young as well as the old will die today.

What Is It All About?

We all have to encounter dying and death—with those we love, and for ourselves. The end of life provides a unique opportunity for us to serve each other, to teach each other, to enjoy immense personal fulfillment and, ultimately, to find serenity and peace—through both the process of dying and being with the dying. Being present for a person who is living the end of life is a privilege and a life-changing experience. Sharing this journey teaches us how to live more fully by being compassionate toward others and ourselves. Many of the people I love will die before I do. I want to learn all I can to support them and then to die peacefully myself.

Loretta Downs, Founder,
Chrysalis End of Life Inspiration

PERHAPS THERE IS more to discover and express as well as choices to be made when dealing with the subject of dying and death than the parameters laid down by officially sanctioned philosophical and religious teachings as well as portrayed in the mass media arena of popular culture and public discourse.

Death is an integral part of living, an inevitable outcome of being alive that brings closure to a life story. Once again, as was the case during birth, we embark on a journey. However, this time to return into the womb of the eternal, where there is relief from the trials and tribulation of embodied existence, where there is no need for pain, fear, striving or sorrow, and where we find union with the deathless source.

What are some of the difficulties and hurdles, physical, mental, emotional and spiritual, likely to be encountered when we face dying and death? Can the dying and death experience present a challenge to the living that can serve to give greater meaning and purpose to life? What did Plato have in mind when he declared: "Those philosophizing rightly are practicing to die?" To be sure, questions serving as valid grounds for inquiry into the nature of dying and death.

However, to place the living/dying experience in an enlarged perspective, let us first give our attention to what occurs before or after death depending on one's beliefs—namely, birth. For, it is also the collective destiny of humankind to be born. And if birth were to be seen for what it truly is at its essence, spirit now possessed by matter, as frightening, difficult, challenging and transformative an experience as the dying process, we might very well ask of ourselves, not are we capable of dying a "good death," but, rather, do we have what it takes to be born into this world and its offerings?

As Stanislav Grof, in *The Ultimate Journey: Consciousness And The Mystery Of Death*, informs us, ". . . during birth we experience physical sensations and emotions often surpassing anything we previously considered humanly possible involving sensations of a severe, life-threatening confinement and a desperate and determined struggle to free ourselves and survive . . . Because birth represents an actually or potentially life-threatening situation, it creates a deep liaison between birth and death in our consciousness. The memory of birth is an important source of fear of death; this explains why reliving birth in the process of psychospiritual death and rebirth can free us from such fear and transform our way of living."

In the realm of birth, we are enticed by the entreaties of this world to be willing to come here for the first time or to return enticed by a mother ready for us who has cast out a net baited with mother's milk held up to the sky by the hands of a father in waiting. Spirit waiting to be embodied now needs to endure the birthing of self as seen with eyes wide open and consciousness expanded so that the curtains of what passes for reality have been lifted in order to witness the awesome, terrifying and wondrous experience that birth truly is.

Nowhere is this journey better described than in *Psychedelic Drugs Reconsidered* by Dr. Lester Grinspoon and James Bakalar, where a psychedelic, a word derived from the Greek term psych-delos meaning mind expanding and enhancing, birth experience is related in a manner that joins shock and awe:

> *After the vulture-mother ordeal, I have the sensation of having died. When MB and WR move my body on the couch, I perceive it as my corpse being placed in the grave. However, I experience the placing of the corpse in the grave as simultaneous with the placing of the egg in the womb.*

It is not death but birth that terrifies me. IK is standing before a frightful tunnel, again the vision of one of those fiery, infernal organs in Hieronymous Bosch's The Garden of Delights . . . Pervasive and total is also the knowledge that man's greatest trauma is birth, not death, that it takes no courage to die but infinite courage to be born.

I have the awful sensation that I have been born an infinite number of times and that I will continue to be born forever and ever . . .

I realize that I must go through the tunnel of birth again and I plead with MB: 'No not again, please. I don't want to be born again. I have been born so many, many times. Why must I be born again?' But I must, she insists. She is very understanding. She is holding me, embracing me, and almost weeping. She so sorry for the pain I will endure, but she cannot help me. I must be born. So I plunge through the birth canal and it is utterly terrifying. Forces are pushing me, squashing me, hairs, mucus, liquids are choking me. I cannot breathe. I will die and disintegrate. I am the little white egg that will be squashed by the claws of contractions. I am suffused with the realization that man perceives his own death (extinction) at the moment of birth. The two processes are inseparable. I cannot breathe. I am being squashed. I feel the pressure of all the mountains of the world, of all the planets. I am a speck that will be obliterated. I am ready to die. At this moment, a tremendous force pushes me through an opening and I am born. Water, piss, blood, milk, semen gush forth and I recognize them all as the same sacred elixir of life. I am being bathed, baptized in this blessed fountain of human sap. I also experience an enormous discharge of energy that I can only very lamely describe as the orgasm of a star . . . The orgasm of a star involves an ecstatic overflow of heat and light that extends the outlines of my celestial body to the vastness of the universe and sends out waves of my power throughout all existence. The ecstasy of this moment is, once again, indescribable. I am transported by the most beatific, blue light of benediction. I feel the music in Bach's Magnificat: Blessed, blessed lamb of God that washes away the sins of the world. I am the Madonna with the Christ Child, both the child and mother at once. I am all the mothers and babies of the world suckling at the breast. The feeling of ecstatic tenderness and fulfillment at this moment is beyond all words.

However, let us remember that it is not a finite I who is being birthed, but the temporal embodiment of a living process in existence prior to the individuated self being formed out of waves of energy. As Einstein taught us, energy, including a life process, can neither be created nor destroyed. It quite simply is. In essence, I am not my body save for a brief moment in time known as a life. I do not exist to any greater degree than a wave has a reality to it other than for the moments between being released from ocean, traveling to shore, and receding into ocean.

Life itself is without end. Death doesn't conclude a life process, although it might end the specific pattern around your life. What merges into the universal at the time of death is wave, as glorious and filled with light as you have fashioned it into being, returning to its source.

Death and Dying Lessons
For Life Enhancement

IT WAS DURING my freshman year at college that I first came upon the afore-mentioned aphorism of Plato's: "Those philosophizing rightly are practicing to die." I defined this to mean, if you wish to live life well, practice dying. However, I was unable to comprehend to any appreciable degree the wisdom contained within these words, and remained unaware of the profound impact they would have on my life, until three events transpired in years to follow that served to redefine who I am and how I would go about living my life.

The first episode occurred in 1965 when I took a leave of absence from the City College of New York during my junior year to join the U.S. Army. Designated a combat engineer, I was trained to be an efficient destroyer of property and to kill on orders without compunction or misgivings. Believing I knew Louis well, I was shocked to discover existing within me lurked a heart of darkness waiting to be unleashed.

It was as if my relationship to self and others, my very consciousness had been possessed by a demon whose view of the world was now also mine. I had allowed myself to be taken into the valley of the shadow of death and left there, where my companions, men in chains filled with grief and despair, stared at each other as they awaited their turn to be led off to butcher others and be butchered in turn.

"There is no way to peace. Peace is the way." These simple yet potent words, spoken by Mahatma Gandhi, posed the challenge I had decided to take on. Surely, not an easy path to walk on given given that the country I loved had decided to, in Orwellian terms, indoctrinate its citizens in the belief that war is peace.

Asking myself, Louis, do you wish to be a messenger of death, I embarked on a journey into my very essence, culminating in a decision to seek release from the U.S. Army active reserves as a conscientious objector, a decision that made me realize I could walk in this world manifesting a heart of light. However, living such a life meant taking a road less traveled. Had I gone off to war and done my duty, rewards were in store for me, perhaps even a medal for taking a life. By deciding not to be willing to kill, I faced the possibility of going to prison.

My encounter with the realm of being a bringer of death forever changed my life, because in choosing life over death I had decided to live life more fully in accordance with a deeper understanding of what it means to be a civilized and humane being. I resolved to make the pursuit of peace and justice one of my central life pursuits, a life choice I have remained true to until this day.

The occasion of the second episode was a Spring day in 1965, when, in order to make my junior year Sociology class at

Highland Park High School, located in Highland Park, Illinois, acutely aware of the effects of war on those who are its victims, I projected graphic images of boys and girls who had come to know what war is truly about all too well onto the screen in my classroom. Within the pages of an issue of *Ramparts* magazine, dedicated to the children of Vietnam, were photographs of Vietnamese boys and girls whose bodies (not to mention minds and souls) had been horribly mutilated as a result of having napalm and white phosphorous rained upon them by artillery shells and bombs coming from the hands of their purported saviors—U.S. armed forces warriors.

Being a high school teacher is very different from being the typical college professor whose teaching responsibilities pale in comparison to research and committee responsibilities and obligations. My schedule called for teaching five classes in a row each day, one class session following another with a relatively short break for lunch close to the end of the day. However, having to eat breakfast of sorts each morning in order for me to be able to catch the train to work in time resulted in my eating lunch during one of the class periods when I was not the central focus of attention, such as during the time my students were viewing a film.

Stumps in place of arms and legs, burned flesh barely covered by scars stilling being formed, faces melted into chests, such were the photographs of children I presented to my students. Their reactions were no different than mine when my eyes first set upon these children who had seemingly been consumed by vessels of destruction unleashed by devils in human form. Gasps of shock, disbelief and revulsion could not be swept away by profusely flowing tears from virtually all the girls and many a boy, save from those who had hidden their faces at the first sign of what they were about to experience as the lesson of the day.

First, second, third and fourth periods came and went. What I had wanted to accomplish had occurred—awareness and disgust, followed by intense discussion of a rational and emotional nature, each class ending with a slightly different version of the same question. What is the nature of our relationship to what we have seen and heard today, to what is being done in our name?

Fifth period. Classroom darkened. Screen pulled down. Overhead projector turned on. Images appeared on the screen. After a few minutes, however, my attention was focused neither on the images projected on the screen nor my students, but on the teacher. With eyes fixed on the faces of the terrified children, I found myself putting food into my mouth with one hand while my other hand manipulated the projector. "Oh, my god," I said to myself, followed by "what has become of me?"

In the process of teaching others and focusing solely on them, I had become, at least in my mind, the student most affected by the lesson of the day. It was as if I were in front of a screen watching a soap opera or an episode of a comedy show rather than real life forces of destruction and death at work. So focused had I been on the effects of what I was attempting to convey to my students, fervently wanting them to open their hearts and minds to the suffering of others that their country was inflicting on the Vietnamese people, unknowingly I had shut Louis down. What other horrors would I be able to be witness to now without feeling anything now that I had become indifferent to viewing the atrocities of war?

Four decades later, I was confronted by a similar question as banner advertisements for cars, jewelry, clothing, credit cards and other artifacts of the material world flowed across the bottom of my television monitor while the remainder of the screen showed homes, government buildings, bridges, tanks and soldiers and collateral damage (aka known as people) during the first Gulf War blown to pieces by planes of the United States Air Force. To my dismay, institutionalized violence had become popular entertainment.

Just as boulders are more likely to be split asunder by drops of water falling on them than by bolts of lightning, souls are more often broken piece by piece as a result of life's daily experiences of a hurtful or indifferent nature than by a big bang. In Dante's version of hell, the lowest level is reserved for those most afflicted by the callings of the Devil. Who are these denizens of the inferno? Humans who remain silent in the midst of voices crying out in need and hands reaching out for assistance to relieve their suffering.

The third event involved metamorphosis whereby my body, encased in a state of rigidity ever since I froze its life force in the process of not allowing myself to attack my father with intention to inflict bodily harm of an extreme nature was unfettered from its shackles, freed from its self-imposed imprisonment, its zombie like living death, by the liberating and life enhancing power of human pleasure.

My father's persona was that of a man filled with anger as a consequence of the soul searing hurt he experienced as a child still very much alive in him, remnants from the past he carried with him during his entire life. Whenever he came home from work, our household would literally vibrate with anxiety and fear in expectation of another one of his rages, which could be set off by virtually anything my mother, brothers or I said or did. Unleashing these furies would leave his family devastated.

Well, there came a day when his rage took the form of screaming at my mother that "If she didn't just shut up, he would kill her." Shouting the word kill as if she were the enemy and this was no longer basic training, but the real thing, once again he turned our apartment into a battleground.

Al, my older brother and I, he twelve years of age and I ten, witnessed this terrifying scene, our voices cried out in unison, "Leave mom alone!" Our father responded, "Don't you tell me what to do. If you say another word, I will kill your mother." Feelings of panic and anger overwhelmed Al and I as we retreated to our parents' bedroom, slamming close the door behind us, unable to stand the horror unfolding before our eyes. Enveloped in a state of impotence, emasculated in the presence of our mother, we grasped the steak knives hidden away should we ever need to use them to defend ourselves against our father and simulated plunging them into our father's body with the full force of a child gone mad.

As my body rocked back and forth, I visualized the "Nazi" in our home standing in front of me as my knife cut his body open, draining the life force from him. In my frenzied state, I continued thrusting at him with the knife until I felt a tremendous jolt to my body in the form of a bolt of lightning striking my spine with such force that it fused together into one rigid mass as if a steel rod had been placed where my flexible spinal column had once been.

Time moves on. However, while mind might forget by virtue of suppression, body does not, expressing on a daily basis what it has experienced in the past in relationship to our very own body as well as to the bodies of those we are connected to. As I went about my life following the traumatic knife wielding experience of my youth, I would often be told, "Louis, you have such a free mind and such a tight body". It was as if my body was stiff as a corpse and placed in a coffin, its life force dormant, perhaps to be awakened, perhaps not. This state of being lasted for years. Neither chiropractors nor yoga classes able to release my spine from its self-imposed prison cell, resulting in a body not being fully alive.

Years later, on a stormy and snowy night in 1965, I offered to give a ride home to a female colleague who taught in the same high school I did in order to spare her from taking public transportation late at night, which can be scary for a female traveling alone. After having chatted about this and that for a few minutes, she surprised me by asking, given the distance we would have to drive to get to her place and the terrible driving conditions, would I mind if she slept over at my apartment? Being the naïve yet gallant person that I was, I took her question at face value and told her yes, no problem. I offered to sleep on the sofa bed in the living room while she slept in my bed.

Well as such arrangements are wont to result in when human heat is turned on, after a few minutes of being in our separate beds, we found ourselves locked in a passionate embrace, kissing fervently as our hands explored the territory of a naked body other than our own. This being my first sexual experience of any depth, yes, at twenty-five years of age, I was still a virgin, I allowed her, who I knew was more experienced than I in the art of lovemaking due to her being married, to be my guide into the discourse of bodies sharing sexual gratification.

Never had I been touched so gently, yet with so much fire. Soon, I forgot who I was. Louis with the rigid body, engaged in the throes of a struggle between this body of mine, out of fear and force of habit, desperately wanting to remain safe behind locked doors, and this body of mine, weary of its imprisonment, wishing to be released from its place among the living dead. In the arms of a lover, I found embodiment of a quite different nature—as a fully alive entity, willing to take the risk of being in my body, of opening myself to the liberating power of Eros in the human body.

Exploding within her, unleashed energy flowed from the base of my spine throughout my entire body. A spinal column fused together by anger on a day many years ago was now flexible, its life force freed from its confinement. I felt loose and supple, able to easily bend forward and backward as well from side to side. My spine had returned to its rightful place and resumed its intended role within my body. The kundalini snake no longed caged, an energetic force now willing and able to do my bidding. Having experienced a whole body orgasmic release, one of the most healing and freeing experiences physically and emotionally a person could be graced with, I felt as if I had been catapulted into outer space where, after being showered upon by starlight, floated down to earth seemingly having undergone a rebirth.

Being a person primarily of mind, Plato could not have imagined that his advice to practice dying in order to be more fully alive was of relevance in the realm of the flesh. He believed that the body distorted truth, serving to distract it from the reality to be found in the realm of the mind. However, body therapy psychotherapists such as Wilhelm Reich and Alexander Lowen stress the need to address both body and mind as an integrated whole, emphasizing the reciprocal relationship of body and mind if healing of a deep and holistic nature is to occur. Their essential teachings: Honor and listen to the body. A body does not lie. It is one of our wisest teachers, a treasure trove of emotional reality to be mined as we go about living our lives.

Yes, a mind is a terrible thing to waste. So is a body. In either case, to do so results in our living partly here and partly in a grave. The best preparation for dying is to fully embrace life. Sex is ultimately about consciousness, about self-discovery and going beyond everyday reality to the place where we experience truth. Sex invites us to come into life, to have the in-body experience. The more we are in our bodies the less fearful we will be of the out of body experience known as death.

In pursuit of the sacred we follow many paths. We travel to consecrated places all over the world, worship gods and goddesses, bow in the presence of the holy, follow numerous and varied disciplines to lead us to the divine, and forget the temple we were graced with at the time of our creation—the human body. We do not need the out-of-body experience to enter the celestial realms of the heavenly. We need only the in-body experience to realize that, above all else save for the earth itself, our bodies are where the most sacred action is taking place.

Each Day A New Beginning

THERE ARE THOSE who, upon confronting mortality, instruct us to protest our demise, to not go like sheep to our deaths, but to scream bloody murder upon sight of the grim reaper in order to drown out the sound of the bell tolling for us. Such raised voices are certainly a most understandable way of viewing the ending of a life. To be alive is indeed a gift from the universe. Do souls not need to experience the reality of existence on earth that they might enjoy the fruits of earthly love and be forged by human struggle into being strong enough to experience the cycle of life and death?

However, as is the case in all human affairs, there exist other doors into the house of dying and death, a primary one being that of acceptance and surrender to life's rhythms and flows. In fact, I was in the presence of such a passageway a few weeks ago as I sat on a bench in my backyard observing hostas merging into the earth for their winter rest before re-emerging in the spring. No fear, no socio-religious-cultural construct to be intimidated by, no resistance. Just doing what plants do naturally—surrendering to the birth/death/birth/death/birth/death . . . cycle, for they travel not in a straight line with a beginning and end, but rather in circles, a truth known to all who exist close to the land or in sight of the vast oceans.

The venerable Buddhist monk and teacher Thich Nhat Hanh speaks of such a reality, informing us that to view our lives in a linear fashion is, in fact, an illusion, a turning away from who we are in truth. Yes there is birth and death, being and non-being. However, he goes on to describe such a worldview as one of waves. A wave seemingly has a beginning and an end. Yet the sea from which it arises is the source of its life, and it has neither beginning nor end.

Whether it be the words of sages and spiritual teachers, or the expressed realizations of the dying and their loved ones, all speak of the incredible value that the nearness of death bestows upon the present moment. Rising from sleep each morning a new day is before us, to live it as if it were the last day of our lives, or to believe with certainty that tomorrow is not just a promise. Yet, albeit it is our desire and intention to have many more days in our lives, so do all those who die each day, including today. Believing we can die this very day is not a morbid thought. To the contrary, it is a life affirming principle, reminding us that all we truly have is the present, that now is the time to live life as if it were indeed our last day. All who have loved and lost know that just to be alive is our most prized possession, a gift to be cherished and shared with others.

To include in our daily life affirming practice a meditation on dying and death offers us a clear mirror in which to see the choices open to us each day, to realize what has meaning and value for us. It compels us to remember not to allow whatever time we have left to be dribbled away, spent on foolish and meaningless pursuits. It heightens the preciousness of those we love because of their mortality. It require of us a willingness to risk pain in committing ourselves to a meaningful attachment to another, to view each other with eyes of compassion, to speak the language of love and to touch each other lovingly as if this were the last day of our lives. It reminds us to bring flowers of various forms to the living as well to the dead. It also reminds us to ask for and accept flowers of various forms from others.

Tales of Dying and Death

Jack's Story I

And What Is The Worth Of A Man

I N THE FALL of this year my father departed along with the autumn leaves, as his aged, weathered and frail body surrendered to the inevitable and went gently into the night. On Friday he suffered a stroke that left him in a coma. On Saturday he died. On Monday he was cremated. Jack, once a vibrant man with life coursing throughout his body, was now ash.

My father, an immigrant from Lithuania in the early 1900's, high school dropout because his father had died and he needed to help support his family, pushcart peddler, candy store owner, manager of a ten-cent-a-dance-dance hall, husband of Yetta, sire of four sons, this entire person, once 5'6" and 160 pounds, was now contained in an urn I could hold in one hand. A quite humbling experience for those of us who wish to see ourselves as the center of the universe.

"Louis, I have some news for you. Your father is dead. He didn't suffer." Such were the words spoken to me by my mother in her usual matter of fact manner when she informed me of my father's demise. As I continued to listen to her words, my mind flashed back to some forty years ago, when a telephone call had informed Yetta of the death of her mother. She put down the receiver, shed a few tears, and proceeded to go about her business as usual. What else could this woman do, herself an immigrant from Poland in the late 1920's with but a second grade education? Barely holding together a family seemingly always on the verge of emotional and financial chaos, her husband being both a tyrant in our home and a compulsive gambler, who had even gone so far as to sell virtually all of their furniture along with her engagement ring to pay off gambling debts while she was in the hospital delivering their first child, what else could a mother do but get her act together, and keep a steady hand as humanly possible on the rudder of such a household?

Our telephone conversation came to an end. I cried. I moaned. I wailed. Jack was a difficult man to have as a father, but he was my father, and I grieved for him, for my loss. Yet, as the days and weeks went by, I was burdened with a pervasive sorrow, a feeling of not having grieved deeply enough for this significant man in my life.

So I called the funeral home in Miami where my father had been cremated, inquiring of its representative as to whether or not his ashes had been placed in the waters of the Atlantic Ocean in accordance with his wishes? The woman to whom I was speaking checked out the status of his remains, and informed me that his ashes had not yet been disposed of. Our ensuing conversation proceeded as follows:

I: "Would it be possible for me to obtain some of his ashes in order for my family to conduct a memorial service for him?"

She: "I'll need to inquire about that. Let me put you on hold while I speak to my supervisor . . . Yes that can be arranged. How much do you want?"

I: "How much of my father do I want? I have no idea. Just a small portion would satisfy my family's needs."

She: "That's too imprecise. We need to know the exact quantity you want."

I: "I really don't know. Just some small amount."

She: "How about $15 dollars worth including postage?"

I: "Yes, that would be fine."

She: "You should have the packet in a week or so along with the billing."

I: "Thank you."

In Arthur Miller's classic American tragedy, *Death of A Salesman*, a tale of a husband and father who was ground to pieces by the demons inside of him as well as by the forces of unbridled capitalism, at least the man has an insurance policy of some meager worth to leave to his family. Had my father's dignity not suffered an even greater depreciation? In a society where a man's worth is defined by the size of his greenback dollar bill roll, he literally could be bought for a paltry fifteen dollars.

Some ten days later, a small package about the size of a standard hardcover book arrived in the mail. My father had been delivered. I placed the unopened package on top of a desk next to some wilted roses, partners on a journey into the beyond. It would not be until Sunday, four days in the future, that the memorial service was to be held. So I went about my business of the day.

Evening came, and I shared with my family the news of my father's arrival. Ana, my daughter, eight years old, wanted to know if she could take the package to school the next day for show and tell? "No," I said. Ben, my son, age three, wanted to know if he could play with the ashes? "No," I said. After all, parents do have to set some limits for their children.

On Sunday my wife, children and I accompanied by my father's remains drove to Lighthouse Beach on Lake Michigan, just a few blocks from our home. After saying our goodbyes to dad and granddad, we released his ashes into the murky blue water. As we were walking back to where our car was parked, my son, Ben, turned towards me and asked, "Dad, are you going to die?" A most understandable fear to be expressed by a three year old, for had not another son, none other than his dad, lost a father.

My answer to Ben's question took this form. I sat down on the sand with my legs spread apart as if the space I had created were a nesting place. Beckoning Ben to join me, I placed his body within the space formed by my legs as we sat face to face. Taking his left hand with my left hand, I placed it against my chest where my heart was beating as if it were a tom tom drum while at the same time I held Ben's right hand in my right hand. Looking directly into his eyes, I said, "Yes, Ben someday I, too, will die. However, just as you feel my beating heart now and the comfort of my body next to yours, I want you to know that no matter where the two of us are, either close or far away, either in this world, or in a world beyond, you will always have my love with you. All you need do is to close your eyes, breathe deeply, open your heart to my presence within it, see me in your mind's eye, and I will be with you in the form of my boundless and endless love for you. Ben do you understand what I am saying to you?"

Ben, with tears in his eyes, said, "Yes, daddy." Tears flowed like rain from the two of us as we hugged each other fervently and deeply as if we might not be this close again.

Having reached out to Ben to assuage his distress, it was now my turn to allow myself to feel my deep sense of loss. I lowered my weary body onto the sand, its coarseness rubbing against my skin reminding me that I was still alive. My father could not hold me, but the earth could, and so could the outstretched arms of my wife, my girl, my boy as they embraced me, enclosing me in a circle of love, the home I had been seeking all my life. I wept and wept and wept, tears held back since I was a child now flowing like a river.

My father had died. I had paid $15 for him. I ask, what is the worth of a man?

Jack's Story II

A few days prior to my father's death, he turned to me and asked, "Louis, my son, do you love me?" Hearing these words, I thought, how dare you ask me such a question, you who were such a difficult father, hurting your children and your wife and the mother of your sons so often and so deeply? However, as I have come to learn during the course of my studies on the subject of and experiences with dying and death, confronting who we are at the deepest core of our beings is what encountering life's endings can, in good part, be all about. That is, asking of ourselves, those departing and those who are left behind, to face difficult and often painful questions and challenges. To reach out beyond the self we know and have grown accustomed to being around and directing our life in order to allow our heart to lead, to be our guide and teacher, to seize the opportunity to make of life a path of heart as well as of mind.

My father's question was his final gift. In reality, he had posed a life affirming challenge to his son: To reflect upon what is the true nature of compassion, forgiveness and love?

Compassion. If compassion is to be a healing force in our lives and in the lives of others, the challenge is to be compassionate to those who, in our eyes, are seemingly undeserving of compassion as well to the deserving. Compassion must go beyond being a noun and a feeling. It must be a verb, an action; in essence, engaged compassion.

Forgiveness. Yes, the more we open ourselves to others, the greater the possibility of experiencing hurt and disappointment of a deep nature. However, no risk, no gain. It is an unlocked heart, not a closed one, which poses the possibility of finding arms to embrace us lovingly.

We also need learn to forgive if for no other reason than we might be forgiven by others. Is there a mother or father who has not/will not hurt one's child, and has not asked/will not ask for forgiveness? Is there a daughter or son who has not/will not hurt one's mother or father, and has not asked or will not ask for forgiveness?

It is necessary to forgive those people who have hurt and disappointed us by not being perfect. If not, the life we live will be filled with emptiness. The truth is that perfect people, albeit an understandable desire, is more than any human being can bring into our lives. Perfect people do not exist, and the cost for not being able to forgive imperfect people is sentencing ourselves to loneliness.

Love. As with compassion, if love is to be a healing force in our lives and in the lives of others, the challenge is to be loving to the unloving and well as to the loving, to send love not only into the light but also into the shadows, to allow the healing force of love to set us free.

The overall lesson to be learned is that the dying experience offers us the opportunity to confront those aspects of ourselves that need to be allowed to die, to be let go of, in order for our higher selves to emerge, and life ahead to be experienced in a state of higher consciousness. This is the great opportunity offered to us when love is the underlying force guiding us in how we relate to the dying and death of others.

Linda Johnsen, writing in *The Living Goddess: Reclaiming the Tradition of the Mother of the Universe*, speaks to such a transformative experience:

"Let's look at another of the mystery religions, the famous Dionysian rites of ancient Greece. At the center of the mystery stands a human woman named Semele, who becomes pregnant by Zeus. Semele dies in childbirth as her son Dionysus is born. But Dionysus is a divine child and restores his mother to life, giving her a new name and taking her to live with the gods. The participants in this 'cult' understood that they were Semele, and that through the grace of God divine awareness was growing within them. The process is terribly painful, because for higher consciousness to be born, the lower self must perish. Once the Higher Self takes birth, however, it illuminates and reintegrates the personality, and life becomes divine."

Yet, as we all know by virtue of our own life experience, it takes disciplined and habitual practice to move from knowing what to do to doing what we know. And so it was the case with the healing journey my father and I embarked on at the time of his dying. The resolution of my relationship to my father was not a fait accompli. He remained ingrained in my emotional life notwithstanding his passing as exemplified in the following excerpts from my diary recorded after his passing.

Memories are stirred up, taking me back to a Thanksgiving holiday of many years ago when I returned home from being away at school to spend the holidays with my family. Before entering their home, I breathed deeply in order to center and place myself in a state of mind that would serve to keep me from being caught up in dreadful remembrances of the past and the mechanical relationship routines of the present.

After dinner was over and as I was about to leave for distant parts, my father approached me in order to shake my hand and say goodbye. Grasping his extended hand with my right hand, I held it firmly, pulled him close to me, put my arms around him as I brought his body even closer to mine, and spoke the unspeakable as far as my home had been concerned, 'Dad, I love you.'

With tears swelling up in his eyes, he extricated himself from my embrace, ran into the bathroom, closed the door, and locked himself inside.

Quietly I walked over to the door and listened. I could hear his fast breathing and deep sobbing. After a few minutes had passed, he came out, and, without saying a word, made it clear to me that all he wanted to do was shake hands and say goodbye. I acceded to his wishes. We shook hands and he went into his bedroom. I stood trembling, not as had always been the case in the past, with anger, but rather with compassionate sorrow, for I felt as if I were in the presence of a frightened and hurt animal, unaccustomed to affection and untrusting of its intent.

I never again felt hate for my father because I now realized that all the crazed and hurtful behavior he had inflicted upon his family, wife and children he loved in theory, but not in practice, originated from a dark, forbidding still raw and excruciating painful part of his being, a childhood from hell that had never healed.

What threatened him most to the depth of his being was love not hate, intimacy not distance. My loving embrace and words opened a door for him into the realm of family relations that was too threatening to his sense of self, to what he had learned to be and do in order to cope with what life had bestowed upon him. In essence, the fabric of his childhood was still ruling his life. He had learned who needs love when it can open you up, make you vulnerable, allowing pain to get in?

*From that moment on, I did not allow my father
to inflict abuse upon me either through word or deed
while in his presence, because it was as much in his best
interests as well as mine that such transgressions not
occur. At the same time, from that moment on, I felt only
compassion for him. I forgave him, and hoped he could
find the strength within himself to forgive me for the
hardness of heart I had shown him up to this point in
our life journey together as my way of protecting myself
from him. After all, he was my father, and children do
want their father's love.*

*   *   *

*I need a bath. As the bathtub fills with hot water and
the aroma of the lemon grass scented incense permeates
the air, I inhale deeply the vapors of the purifying oils of
pine and eucalyptus placed in the water that I may be
cleansed and released from any of my father's negative
karma I have either inherited or imbibed during our
time together when I was his young son and he was the
resident father tyrant in our home.*

*I visualize my father's energy being transformed into
fuel to be used to empower those who feed the hungry,
clothe the naked, heal the sick, and minister to the
spiritually impoverished. With such thoughts I release
him, sending him off into the light.*

*After drying myself off, I massage a blend of sweet
almond, coconut, and vanilla oils onto my body as a
libation to the gods. Placing three drops of anise oil*

on my heart to release forgiveness, and three drops of lavender oil on my third eye that I may set the two of us free from all entanglements of pain, resentment and hate lest his heart and mine be forever plagued and entwined with such hurts, I face the sun, cup my hands to catch sunlight, and offer this gift to my father as his soul makes its way from here to wherever its destination might be.

It is time for me to move on beyond what was to what is. It is time for me let go of the past and live in the present moment. It is time for his heart and mine to be broken open to forgive each other and to allow the cleansing and healing power of love to wash away all that which keeps us apart. It is time for father and son to be father and son.

Ben's Story

On a day when Ben was either four or five, I lost it in the form of a temper tantrum that left my wife, daughter and son hurt and trembling with fear. Emerging from the darkness within my inner being, as if I were once again possessed by wounds and rage I had known as a child, was a part of myself that left me feeling out of control, guilty and ashamed. Not knowing how else to keep my family from having to experience this side of me in the future, for this was not the first time they had been in the presence of a husband and father seemingly gone mad, I yelled out in a thunderous voice, "I'm leaving and not coming back."

Paula and Ana had fled to an upstairs bedroom in order to escape from my unleashed furies, but Ben, eyes filled with tears, remained sitting on the stairway. As I was about to go out the door, I heard a pleading voice, "Dad, please don't leave! Please don't leave! I don't think I can live without you."

My heart was deeply pierced by the sound of his pleading voice and words, allowing the love contained within it to flow freely again as it washed away the wounds and rage and brought me to my senses. A child's greatest fear is abandonment, perhaps akin to a dying person's fear of separation and being alone. These were my loved ones, my life's treasures, how could I have given myself permission to be so destructive to my wife and children? "Never again," I vowed could this occur.

Filled with repentance, I walked over to Ben and sat down next to him. Tears filled my eyes as we held each other tightly. "Ben, I want us to do something that will help me to keep a promise I made to myself never to hurt Mom, Ana and you in this way again, and never to threaten to leave you. Will you trust me and do this for me?" "Yes, poppa," he replied

In a moment or two, I returned holding a safety pin that I had sterilized using the flame of a match. "Ben, I want to take a vow that I will never again threaten to leave you. I know how much my doing so makes you feel scared and sad. I want this to be a blood vow because this is the strongest of promises and is more likely to last. I am going to stick this pin into my finger until we can see a drop of blood. I also want to stick the needle into your finger until a drop of blood appears. Then, as I vow never again to threaten to leave you, we are going to press our fingers together to mix our blood. Once we do that, both you and I will always remember this day and this vow. Is this ok with you?"

"Ok, poppa. Let's do it. But can I close my eyes when you stick the needle in my finger?" "Yes," I replied, "but keep your heart open."

On that day, a necessary death had occurred. I had put a remnant from the past, a part of me that I needed to let go of, to sleep. However, I did not want "it" to rest in peace, to "reincarnate" should life's circumstances send out a siren call for its emergence. It was now up to me to do the necessary therapeutic and spiritual work, not so much to bury the wound and rage in the deepest of graves, but to transform such energies into fuel to be used to keep me reaching out to others when I or they are in need of a little help from a friend to get by.

Joe's Story

Joe, I Hardly Knew You

My father, Jack, died in the fall of 1991 at the age of eighty-nine, an old man. Joe, his son, one of my kid brothers, died in the Winter of 1992, just nine months later, at the age of forty-eight, a young man.

Joe, in accordance with our family's genetic pool, had long eyelashes, the kind that many a woman would die for. I had never noticed their exquisite beauty until I gazed down at him as he lay dying on a hospital bed. His eyelashes caught my attention because, save for a wisp of very fine hair on his scalp, and a couple of days worth of stubble on his face, his chemotherapy had resulted in the loss of virtually all of his body hair; he who had once been graced with such a luxurious mane.

A day later my brother was in the light, having passed on due to a body so ravaged by cancer and so wracked by pain that death came as a blessing both to him and his family. His caring and empathetic doctor asked, "Joe, do you want to go to sleep?" All my brother uttered in response was one word, and yet this one word expressed everything needed to be said. The word was, "Please."

Hour by hour, the dosage of intravenous morphine entering his body was increased, resulting in an ever-decreasing respiration rate. No pain, no gain, is a saying that belongs to the living. No pain, much gain, is a sweet calling to the dying. Joe went quietly into the night, his wife holding and stroking one hand while I held his other hand and stroked his forehead gently and soothingly as if he were a baby about to fall off into sleep. He died. We cried tears of sorrow and of relief. There is just so much living and just so much dying we can take before our weary bodies need to rest. As we bore witness to this young man dying, seemingly well before his time according to the rational order of human affairs, his passing served as a reminder to all present, mortal beings that we are, that our day of final goodbyes would also come to pass.

Joe, I hardly knew you. You were seemingly always somewhere else other than in the family living quarters. Why not with six people sharing three and one-half rooms plus a bathroom without a sink, the apartment's one washbasin located in the kitchen, to be used for the washing of humans as well as for cooking and eating utensils, resulting in very crowded space? The streets were your life where you constantly looked for room to breathe and for action. Before we knew it, you had dropped out of high school, an integral part of the ritual of becoming a "man" in our part of town. Having reaffirmed your choice of life on the streets as your mode of existence, little did you know at the time that this would be a life path that you were to continue to follow into adulthood, making your living as a vendor at flea markets, just like dad who used to peddle his wares of fruits, vegetables and plush dolls from a pushcart.

A boy growing up amidst the slum of Brooklyn, New York, you did what you felt was needed to make it with the boys—respect and fellowship, and with the girls—awe and sex. In the process you became a most adept gangbanger, utilizing a car's antennae to whiplash your opponents into pain and submission. Did you not always admire Zorro, a swordsman par excellence, as he swashbuckled his way into our home every evening via the miracle of television?

Then came the U.S. navy. Off you went, far away from the tenements of your upbringing, where you had lost sight of who you were as you became caught up in a street life drama of youthful passion, exuberance and tragedy captured so very well in *West Side Story*. I had hardly known you, your life interests and mine rarely jibing, and now you had sailed off beyond the horizon. To no one's surprise, the navy and you never really made it, what with you going AWOL a number of times, winding up in the brig, a merry-go-round ride finally resulting in an early, albeit honorable, discharge from the armed services. However, after having left home and experiencing a strong taste of freedom, you were not about to return. So, you found yourself a wife, sired four children, one of whom, your only son, was to die when still a child in a tragic automobile accident, a loss that resulted in a part of your life force also dying, a loss that never left you, a loss that broke both your heart and spirit.

You divorced your wife, and played around with the ladies until a new special woman came into your life. You married her, becoming a family of seven, she having had two children by a previous marriage to a member of the Hells Angels, who was currently doing time in prison. You and your family went on the road, selling your wares at various and sundry flea markets across America, truly an American family on the move.

Standing still, staying in one place for any appreciable period of time, simply was not in your cards until those headaches turned out to be a cancerous brain tumor. Now, no longer on the go, you remained in one place except when a hospital attendant would crank your bed up or down. As the days, weeks, and months, not many, March through August, went by, increasingly so you began to look like dad in his final days, heavily wrinkled skin, all hunched up, almost fetal like and yet resembling a wizened old geezer at the same time. All that you wanted was to be warm, sleep, and without pain. You cried a lot, more than you did your entire life unless you count the deeply felt but unseen weeping of life's hurts and tragedies within you as tears.

We became close in your final days. We talked most intimately. We held hands and each other. We looked into each other's eyes and rediscovered a love not seen since we were children. No matter how many tears were shed between us, we could not wash away the reality that you, kid brother, son, husband and father, were dying. Off you went into a coma, now and then coming out of it for a moment or two, gesturing with your hands for someone to be near to you, to touch you, to hold you, until you succumbed to death's calling.

Now you lay in the earth next to Mikie, your sweet young boy. Whenever you visited the cemetery where he had been buried, you comforted son and father alike by letting him know that one day the two of you would be back together joined for eternity.

At the moment of your death, I envisaged/saw (what is truth?) you leaving your body to ascend into the clouds where our father and your son were waiting as they held out their inviting arms to take you in. A smile lit up your face as tears of sorrow gave way to tears of joy. How could it be otherwise? The guys were back together again.

Within a relatively brief period of time, I had lost a father and brother, and my young son had lost a grandpa and uncle. When my father died, Ben turned to me and asked if I were going to die? Holding Ben tightly against my chest, I told my boy that someday the time would come for me to pass on, but to remember that I will always be with him in his heart.

On our way back home from scattering my brother's ashes into the waters of Lake Michigan, my son inquired of me once again if I were going to die? I took him into my arms, and, gazing intently into his eyes, I said, "Yes, I will . . ." Before I uttered another word, Ben looked intently into my eyes, and said, "Daddy, when you die, all I need to do is close my eyes, open my heart, and your love will be with me always."

Yes, amidst the sorrow, life's precious moments sprout forth like an early spring flower blooming during the cold of winter. Maybe, I too, will go gently into the night, now that I know that the ultimate miracle of love is that love is given to us to give to one another, both here and in the beyond.

Joe, my dear brother, rest, be in peace, always remember that you are loved and you are known, never to be forgotten.

Mikie's Story

Joe and Mary, his first wife, now confined to a health care facility as she deals with mental trauma and physical disabilities, finding themselves caught up in one of those kinds of marriages in which make war not love passes for discourse, are engaging in an exchange of words marked by lower brain ferocity and low blow emotional barbs that cut through their defenses, wounding each other deeply. Gathering her four young children, Mary stormed out of the house, got into the car, so blinded by her anger she neglected to place seatbelts on her children, ran a red light, was hit head on by an oncoming car, and the horror ensued.

Mary was hurt, seemingly not too seriously at the time, but which would prove more severe as time went on. Susan (15), Sharon (13) and Samantha (7) suffered major bodily injuries, but were destined to recover. Mikie (9), my brother's only son, was killed instantly upon impact.

"Do not cry," my brother was told. "Think positively. Your son is with God in heaven." Such are the words of well-intentioned fools or expressions of ignorance. "My son, my little boy is dead, and I am not supposed to cry, to just get over it? I do not wish such a fate on any other father or mother. However, unless you experience the loss of a child as I have known it, you do not have the slightest idea of what I am going through, what I have to contend with each day." Such were the thoughts going through Joe's mind.

In times of seemingly unbearable misfortune, we are here to serve the needs of those who are hurting; to extend our arms in offerings of support; to listen, not judge, or give advice unless asked to. Compassion to relieve the suffering of others is the church bell calling out to us at these times.

However, always remember that compassion takes two forms. Sometimes, what is called for is compassion of such a nature as to take a specific action to relieve the suffering of the person who is dying. At other times, what is called for is compassion of such a nature as to be there to serve the person who is dying, but this time in stillness. Just as mothers and fathers minister to their children by virtue of their presence as well as by their actions, ministering to the dying also includes the gift of just being present, a communion of the kind of deep interconnected stillness that makes it clear to the dying as well as to the living that there is no separation, no abandonment when we live or after we die. How can it be other than so when in the stillness we became as one?

Mikie's body was buried in the earth. Mikie's soul lived on in my brother's heart. However, to my brother the presence of his son's soul did not lift up his spirits. To the contrary, Joe continued to be weighed down by the belief that Mikie was now just soul because in some way he had contributed to his son's death. Joe's heart was now heavier, overflowing with pain and grief. And a heavy heart is a difficult burden to bear.

Now father and son are back together again. Is this a happy ending? I think not. Life can be very sad at times.

Edward's Story

"Louis, I'm going to die." Those were the words greeting me when I picked up the ringing telephone to hear Eddie, my youngest brother's shaky voice. "I've been diagnosed with a fatal illness, amlyodosis, for which there is no cure. How I got it, I don't know? All I know is that the doctor told me once you contract it, you have anywhere from six months to two years at the most to live."

A Tree Called Edward

The summer of 2005 had been a most wonderful one for my family, brimming with the joys of living the good life, until the time of Edward's, my youngest brother, dying and death arrived.

"How can this be?" This was the question his loved ones ask of God, of man, of woman, of child, of all of creation. The answer to this Job like inquiry is either one of an empty and forlorn silence, the abode of loss and hurt abiding in our beings and souls, or of a full and pregnant stillness, which calls forth the serenity abiding in our beings and souls even amidst life's tragedies.

It was the evening of the day after my brother's death. My good friend Michael and I were sitting on the beach having completed our tai-chi practice. Gazing up at the sky, my eyes were drawn to an especially brightly shining star. Iridescent in nature, I felt as if its lustrous essence were reaching out to touch me.

Feeling as if I were in the presence of Edward, the stillness was broken by a voice seemingly coming from above me, "Louis, I love you." My dear brother was speaking to me. In return, I said to him, "Edward, I love you." These bonding words continued to be exchanged between the two of us to the point that they assumed the form of an intoxicating chant.

The energy of the chanting lifted me higher and higher until I found myself floating among stars searching for Edward, but he was nowhere to be found. I took this to mean that the time for us to be together again had yet to come for me. Both he and I knew that in the name of our family, I had more work to do and love to experience to make the Silverstein heritage to be passed on to the children of our children lighter and lighter.

I have learned from experience that the element of choice is ever present in our consciousness in relation to how we respond to life's transitions, such as the death of a loved one. If I am to heal from this wounding of my mind, heart and soul, I must allow myself to grieve in a manner true to who I am and what I am feeling even if that means transgressing cultural norms. For the truth of the matter is that when I was in communion with Edward on the beach that night, I was immersed in a harmonious serenity, not sorrow.

A very sunny and warm day is blessing my brother's home. Teresa, his wife, two sons, Zack and Logan, Al, my older brother and his wife, Barbara, my son, Ben, and I are driving down from Haleakala after having cast my brother's ashes into the crater, uniting him with eternity. Ben also had grasped some of my brother's ashes in his hand and tossed them into the wind. Ashes joining dust existing since time immemorial as he expressed to uncle Edward his love for him, wishing him "good traveling in heaven."

I shall never forget these moments. Neither shall my son.

Our family and Edward's family, joined by two of Edward's closest friends, Chitron, destined to also die just a few years later, and David, and Yetta, our mother, are now on the road heading toward the Pacific Ocean. Once again, a brother is to be tossed to the wind, to settle into sand and water, becoming one with earth and sea.

My son's kayak, with Chitron as his companion, overturns close to the shore, causing Ben to smile and break out laughing as this turn of events fills him with joy. Edward must be around, for he always liked to bring a smile and laughter to a child.

I will never forget these moments. Neither shall my son.

Six o'clock in the evening of the same day. Edwards's bon voyage party is in full swing, and the time has arrived for the planting of the tree, the roots of which will feed on what is left of my brother. A starfruit tree, placed next to the lotus pond he built, will serve as a living memorial to his once having graced the planet. The tree of Edward is joining the tree of Jack and the tree of Joe, both of which he had helped place in the earth. More of the guys will be back together again.

All who wish to participate, family friends and neighbors, are invited to place some of Edward's ashes on the roots of the tree. Most do so accompanied by a prayer, a mantra, a flower, including the many children who also give thanks it is not their father who is being planted in the earth.

I will never forget this day. Neither shall my son.

It is the late afternoon of the day that my son and I will be returning to our home. Teresa and I are sitting on the porch as we take in the tree of Edward. With tears filled with tears and a broken heart, she faces me and says, "This is overwhelming. I just can't believe it. I know this is just a bad nightmare that I am going to wake up from and Eddie will be home in the morning. He was just a baby, just growing up. I can accept that he has embarked on a cosmic journey, but who am I to lie down on the grass or share my bed with? Who will make breakfast for the kids as I go off to work? Who will be at my side when the going gets rough? I thought for sure we had at least another year or two together. I wanted to be with him at the end, to say goodbye for the last time, to look into his eyes before he left. I miss him so much."

Such are the truthful and soulful words of a wife whose husband always kept her interested, which is no mean trick as marriages move from the years of springtime to the years of fall. There is nothing left to say. Tears flow. After a few moments, the tears wash away the pain and grief, at least for a moment or two.

I take Teresa's hand in mine and go for a walk in paradise. Sitting on a stone bench next to a lotus pond, close to the tree in which my brother is planted, we gaze at the land that Edward and Teresa transformed into a Garden of Eden. I mention to my sister-in-law that Edward's leaves are drooping. He needs some watering. It begins to rain. The tree of Edward is vibrant with life.

I have and will continue to cry rivers of tears in the days, months and years to come. I loved and love my baby brother deeply. We were and are as much soul brothers, kindred spirits, as we were brothers in the flesh. I feel his presence, but I miss his physical body sitting next to mine on a hillside overlooking the ocean, breathing in this serene and peaceful moment in our lives as well as our hopes and dreams for the future.

Yet, my journeys beyond the veil of everyday consciousness into lands that some say do not exist, but that I know always have been and will be, often accompanied by my brother, have taught me that death is neither closure nor final, neither where life ends nor nothingness prevails. Edward, as is true for each of us, was and is made of the stuff of stardust. Although a body comes to an end, what it is composed of at its essence does not. Stardust to body to stardust is our common journey.

My dearest brother, be it in the eternal or in lives to come, we will meet again. I love you.

Edward's Last Letter To Al

Dear Al,

Let's not ask why. It's what is. I'm not writing this because I've given up hope of recovery, only because I have things to say to you I might never verbalize. Even when I recover I could get hit by a bus so why wait.

Please don't be mad or angry because this has happened. I'm not nor am I afraid. Death is part of living, the natural order and can come at anytime. I don't have time to fear the inevitable.

My life has been blessed in many ways, way beyond the ordinary. As you are fond of saying, remember 25 years ago in Britain. Who would have dreamed of such an amazingly beautiful outcome? I've been living a dream these past years, a most wondrous time. A large part of which is because you my brother and all you've done for my family and me. I thank you and love you immensely.

One of the things that have filled me with great joy has been the changes in you. Your relationship with Barbara is something so wonderful for all of us. It has allowed you to begin the difficult journey to escape the legacy of our parents, our family. I've done my part to help purge the shit we were all saddled with. I will leave this life (whenever) lighter and clearer than our parents and my children brighter still. Your part is not over and I refuse to allow you to use my circumstance as a reason to struggle less on your journey of discovery. I will be watching. Life is good, nothing less.

My family and I will need your strength in the days and years to come. I know you will be there for us as you always have. Please come with only good things in your heart and mind. We all deserve only the best.

Aren't we lucky we got to share our lives. We must thank Jack and Yetta for that.

With all of my love to you and Barbara.

Edward

Yetta's Story

During an interchange between my mother and I three years prior to her passing at a party celebrating Yetta's ninety-first birthday, she turned to face me and spoke these words, "Louis I have seen the rope hanging down from heaven, and I know if I climb up the rope, I will be going to heaven. But I don't want to go because I am afraid I will meet your father and my father. I want to see my mother Eva, and my sons Eddie and Joe, but not them."

Yetta not wanting to see her husband was a desire I could understand. My father was both tyrannical and verbally abusive, even going so far as threatening to kill her and all her children more than once during his many rages. However, why my mother would not want to encounter her father was something I could not fathom. I remember him as being an inwardly drawn pious elderly man adorned in his tallis (ritual shawl), worn around his shoulders, and his tefillen (two small leather boxes containing biblical verses), wrapped around his arm, while he sat in a rocking chair reciting prayers from his siddur (Jewish prayer book).

Life on planet earth has taught me that asking why can take you anyplace, irrespective of whether or not you want to go there, but I was not prepared for as well as shocked to hear Yetta's answer to my question, why not your father? I learned Issac was a sexual abuser, who, on more than one occasion, had entered the bedroom of her sister to visit upon this little girl the horrors of a father invading his child's body. Driven by a hard cock having no conscience, a crazed male once again inflicting torture on those weaker than himself as he violated innocence on his journey into the heart of darkness.

When my mother informed her brothers of Isaac's transgressions, with voices spewing anger and minds filled with a murderous rage, they told their father in the strongest terms possible that if he ever committed such an evil deed again, he would not see the light of another day. What is it about the human species that within the very same person there exists the possibility to soar to the heavens as well as descend into hell?

"Ok mom, I will guide you to a place of safety." Grasping my mother's hand firmly while looking into her eyes, the mirror of our souls, and, with a gentle but reassuring voice, told her, "You don't have to be afraid. You, and you alone, are in charge of your journey into heaven. You will meet only those who you wish to be with." She replied, "How do you know this?" I responded, "Mom, I know. Just believe me."

Tears not generated by fear but of relief filled her eyes. We embraced, holding each other as if only death could do us apart, a reality to be experienced all too soon.

Yetta, A Mother's Life

Once upon a time, not very long ago, there lived, in a three and one-half room apartment on the fourth floor of a walk-up tenement building in Brooklyn, New York, Yetta, an immigrant from Poland, Jack, an immigrant from Lithuania, and their four sons, Al, Louis, Joe and Edward.

Yetta came to America in 1927 with the other women of her family, joining the men folk who had emigrated five years earlier; found work in the garment industry, and soon advanced to become a floor leader for the ILGWU (The International Ladies

Garment Workers Union); regularly attended the Rainbow Theater, where ten cents bought you an admission pass and a raffle ticket that one night contained the winning number, a number that, as fate turns, was also held by another theater patron, who, upon casting his eyes on beautiful Yetta, asked her out on a date, wooed her, and finally convinced her to marry him despite his reputation in the neighborhood of being a somewhat unsavory character; and gave birth to four boys who were her pride and joy.

Yetta toiled through the night and early morning to get her children off to school and/or work, which was no easy task given that their home contained only one sink, with the bathroom consisting of but a tub and toilet, to meet the demands of six people; did the laundry by hand and pressed everyone's clothes so that her family would present itself well in the larger world; visited the bakery at the break of dawn each morning come rain, shine, or snow to get fresh bagels and kaiser rolls for her hungry men to devour at breakfast; prepared lunches of kosher salami on wonder bread, or peanut butter and jelly on wonder bread for her men to take to school or work; and made sure there was food on the table for dinner, one more challenging task given that Jack often bet and lost his wages for the week on the horses, forcing her to ask for handouts from local merchants who knew that Yetta would always make good on what she owed; and led rent strikes against a landlord who believed that his tenants, Jews, blacks and Latinos, really didn't' require heat and hot water throughout the entire winter.

Yetta received a telephone one day to hear that her mother had died causing tears to flow for a moment or two, the only time in her life her children ever saw her cry, before getting herself together to continue on with life's responsibilities and chores; regularly took her children to the zoo and to the beach because life was to be enjoyed as well as endured; took great pride in her Brooklyn famous chicken soup laced with sugar, just one the many ways she attempted to counteract the bitterness all too present in the world; made sure that her sons did their homework every night, but this didn't prevent her from losing her two youngest sons to living life on the streets; somehow got it together to move her family to a first floor apartment in a nicer neighborhood, where life was not as rough and less threatening for her boys, and where she didn't have to walk up four flights of stairs a number of times each day, a task that was getting increasingly difficult what with her varicose veins getting worse.

Yetta sent her children out into the world with the knowledge that if she could make it, so could they, and with the belief that humans are here to help lift each other up; retired to the social security haven of Miami Beach with its warmer climate to live out her golden years; endured the death of her husband, all of her brothers and sisters, and two of her sons, yet continued to laugh and enjoy life as she always had in the moments allowed to her and the ones she carved out in between the harshness and disappointments that life offers unto the brave and the decent and the hard working, the salt of the earth; kept on smiling as she bore witness to her body wither and her mind beginning to wander, and took her last breath on a winter night in January.

Yetta, above all, wanted her sons to be educated and to find a woman who would be the love of their lives, which each did, and was also so happy that three of her sons had turned out to be such good fathers, and the other such a good uncle to his brothers' children. Yes, she wanted such blessings of the universe to be visited upon her sons, but to tell the truth, all this is icing on the cake of life for each of us. I say this because I will always remember the words we exchanged the last time I saw her alive.

Yetta: "I was a good mother. You never starved."

Louis: "No mom," I said, "not only did we never starve. We were loved."

Al's Story

1938. Not an exceptionally good year to be born into this world if you were a Jew. As if, to paraphrase the words of John Dos Passos, the struggle for the basic physical necessities of life—not to be hungry, not to be clothed, not to be without shelter were not enough of a challenge, this being a year during the Great Depression, a Jewish child and his parents also had to contend with not to be afraid of the gentiles. When Jack and Yetta were young, the Cossack hordes in Poland and Lithuania were on the warpath terrorizing Jews. Now the anti-Semites in the form of the Nazis and their cohorts were once again wreaking violence on the chosen people.

However, often to survive, one needs to make the best of any situation, for none us were ever promised that existence on this planet would be a rose garden without thorns. The truth of the matter was that there were compensatory factors of a positive nature at play n 1938, enticing Al into becoming spirit embodied in matter.

After all, there was farina cereal creamy style and fresh bagels or Kaiser rolls for breakfast; chopped chicken liver with boiled potatoes and warmed up canned green beans or peas for lunch; and for dinner, Yetta's famous chicken soup, not to mention her matzoth meal and egg battered veal cutlets accompanied by out-of-this world French fries, all to be washed down by Jack's contribution to a satisfying meal—a glass of cold milk spiked with a touch of Pepsi Cola. And for desert, a yankee doodle cupcake or devil dog, both consisting of a cream filled chocolate cake, or jello, or chocolate pudding topped with whipped cream.

Although Paula and I believed there would be time left to be with Al at least once more prior to his passing, such would prove not to be the case. Mind wishing to control body desired not to die, at least not until reaching the age of seventy, just seven months away. However, there comes a time, when body says to mind, "I have given it a good try, but I am so tired, so worn out, no longer in possession of the necessary strength to keep on chasing after symptoms of the illness. I need to rest. I need to be let go of."

Al died quickly taking all of those dear to him somewhat by surprise. Only he knew to what extent the suffering he was experiencing, from the cancer itself as well as from the chemotherapy and radiation therapy wreaking havoc on his body, was too much to bear. The call of the world beyond bodily existence was now for his ears to hear as it had been for his father, mother and two brothers. Al was returning to the source from which he had sprouted some sixty-nine years before.

I had thought that there would be time for Al and I to continue a conversation he had initiated during my last visit with him prior to his death. However, one of life's truths was in play. All we have is today. There is no guarantee of tomorrow. So, I wrote what I had planned to share with him in my journal if only to serve as a reminder of what I needed to do during the time I have left to get my relationship house in order as I come to terms with the ending of my life.

Al, dying is a time for forgiveness of others for hurts and disappointments inflicted on you by others, and for forgiveness of self for hurts and disappointments inflicted on others by you. It is also a time for compassion; that is, to see others and self through compassionate eyes, and to realize that there but for fortune go I. Each of us do the best we can given what we came into this world with and have to contend with during our lifetimes.

Having realized this, I want you to imagine / visualize that standing right in front of you is Jack, your father. What do you want to say to him and what do you want to hear from him as your final gifts to each other?

Al, now Joe is standing right in front of you. What do you want to say to him and what do you want to hear from him as your final gifts to each other?

Al, now Yetta, mom, is standing right in front of you. What do you want to say to her and what do you want to hear from her as your final gifts to each other?

Al, now Eddie is standing right in front of you. What do you want to say to him and what do you want to hear from him as your final gifts to each other?

Al, now I am standing right in front of you. What do you want to say to me and what do you want to hear from me as our final gifts to each other?

Al, now Barbara, your wife, is standing right in front of you. What do you want to say to her and what do you want to hear from her as your final gifts to each other?

Finally, Al, now Al, your very own self, Al, is standing right in front of you. What do you want to say to him and what do you want to hear from him as your final gifts to each other?"

I sit with my eyes fixed on the wind blown flickering memorial candle as if it were a life itself filled with vibrant movement and energy. Soon the flame will cease to be palpable to the eye, its essence transmuted into atoms of smoke that will dissolve into the ether. In similar fashion, the essence of Al, no longer observable to the eye, soul now free of body, journeyed into the light, returning to his origins.

Once again, it is time to say to a brother: Good traveling in heaven.

Barbara's Eulogy To Al

When Al found out that the cancer had gone to his brain—this was back in April—he came up with a quip to accompany the news. He'd tell people about this dire development of his disease and then, quickly add, 'Well, the good news is I finally have documented proof that I have a brain! I have a paper, signed by a doctor. Can you say the same?'

As he spoke, I watched the faces of countless people shift from expressions of consternation and discomfort to uncertainty. I watched them look to Al to guide their reactions, look him in the eyes. And I watched most of them relax. And smile. Of course! He was joking! They could deal with the news then. They could deal with him.

It occurred to me later that Al was using a process he'd devised many, many years ago to handle adversity. No—not handle—overcome. As long as he was on this earth, he would laugh and get others to laugh with him. Yes, sometimes he went overboard. And sometimes you (certainly I!) didn't feel like laughing along. But his invitation was always open. You could join him at any time. What a blessing his presence was. In the words of one friend, 'When Al arrived, you knew the party had begun!'

I was witness to his enormous strength, courage, and dignity throughout the last 18 months of his life. And I tell you—he didn't falter. He was Al Silverstein to the very end.

Having come up with his joke, his 'documented proof,' he used it on everyone—friends, family, acquaintances, and total strangers. That was Al, saying as always, to the last, 'Here I am. This is who I am and how I am. I am not my disease. I am not my doom. My brain, while under attack, is still working, and I will use it to the last. You will look me in the eye. I am the man. Laugh along with me! At life! To life! While we're here together now!'

Here's to you Al! I'm grateful for your life, wit, and grace.

Louis's Story

My story began on March 7 1940, the day my mother gave birth to her second son in Greenpoint Hospital, Brooklyn, New York. The doctor was late, so two nurses, abiding by hospital rules and regulations in force at the time, grasped my mother's legs firmly and crossed one leg over the other, obviously determined to keep me from coming out until he arrived. If the doctor weren't in attendance, this baby would just have to wait.

Once my mother's legs were let go of, I shot out like a bolt of lightning, Finally, I am, but probably wondering either where am I or what I am I doing here? I might also ask from what glacier, what boulder, what vegetation, what insect, what animal did those particles emanate from that would coalesce and end up being me? Or before life even appeared on our planet as it underwent metamorphosis from stardust to what we call earth, where were those elements now known as me? Am I to be traced back to the time when the universe emerged from space?

The answer that rings true for me is that my history is one with the history of the universe. From the void where nothing exists and all exists, stars were created, fiery cauldrons containing the atoms that make up our world were formed. In the beginning, the earth was not the earth. It was all fire. The rains came in seemingly endless torrents, cooling the earth, giving form and shape to the molten mass. Millions of years later, in sun heated crucibles made of water and salts, a hot broth formed, the primaeval soup, from which minuscule seeds of matter scattered like angel dust in the wind, taking root everywhere, blanketing earth with life's offspring, microscopic eggs filled with energy and matter would form trees, flowers leopards, butterflies and even me.

Life is like a body of water in motion. Within the present there exists the past and the future, the way seed contains tree and apple, apple contains seed and tree, and tree contains seed and apple. All that ever was exists right now. Using such logic, one could look at a life span as a series of ongoing reincarnations. The principle behind each reincarnation being it is the birth of a new self, emerging after those parts of self inhibiting the life force from flowing strongly and freely within us are let go of; that is, allowed to die. When these "past lives" lived within the span of one lifetime are shed, space is created for higher aspects of self to occupy, serving to orient us in the direction of the continuation of soul growth to be manifested on the plane of earthly existence.

A child, restless and questioning. A wonder tree plant. A stranger in a strange land. When I was a young boy at play in the fields of the child's world, I had no concept of what was possible or impossible, acceptable or unacceptable. I went about my life as the spirits moved me. The world of grownups, also known as normal society, didn't seem to mind at first. I'm still not sure why? Perhaps because I was so darned cute, or because the big people viewed me as too small and powerless a creature amidst the constructs of society for anything I believed or did to have an effect on the world anyway.

Whatever the reason, save for when my father was around, which wasn't all that often due to his working a day as well as an evening job, I loved doing mostly what I felt like doing, albeit some of my actions occurred in my secret world. It was exhilarating! Every atom in my body was aflame with the fire of life. Until I went to school, I knew little of expectations, so I never feared that I might disappoint. Between the time I awakened in the morning and time I went to sleep at night, I lived to the fullest in every moment.

Some would say such a blissful existence I speak of exists only due to ignorance and inexperience. Soon, they knew, I would come to realize that the world is a scary, unforgiving, horrible place, and my accepting such a reality was only a matter of time. What they knew for certain was what the future had in store for me would be to join their ranks and become one of the crowd. To fulfill their destiny plan for the likes of me and others of my kind, they began to drill lessons into my head once they were done viewing me as being adorable, no longer their plaything. Here are a few of them: "Everyone is out to get you, to take advantage of you, so put on your armor and strike first." "Play it safe." "Respect authority." "Do what you are told." "Questioning leads to trouble." Get the other guy before he gets you." "Might, riches and work are your most valuable possessions." Over time, these lessons I was being instructed in broke my spirit and caused my zest for life to dwindle. I was being initiated into the ranks of the living dead.

Then one day something happened. It dawned on me that those lessons couldn't be what life is about, because if they were, I wouldn't be so troubled. I wouldn't feel as if I were being suffocated. I knew that life wasn't about the utopia of the child's world, but it isn't about the psychological and spiritual assault we experience during our formative years either. I came to realize that I had made a mistake, for I did not trust my own thoughts and feelings. I had my own brain and heart for a reason.

Many people desire great wealth, but I think that is too small of a dream. From the very beginning of my existence, I had an answer to life's questions and callings. I was going to fly away. What did I have to lose? Off I went—out of place, out of body, out of mind. Many years later after much heartache, I learned the cost of searching for who I am among the stars. I didn't see you, so intent was I on finding myself. However, my guardian angels in the form of those who loved me and an earth that continued to nurture me turned Louis around. I came to the realization that if I were to fulfill my destiny, I needed to be in-body, not out of body; that interconnectedness, not separation, was my path to a highly realized and fulfilled life.

There is no one way to live. There is no one way to die. Each dying person takes their life experiences into their dying. As we live, so shall we die. Yet, to live and to die have something in common. A life filled with pain and fear is no way to live. An ending of a life filled with pain and fear is no way to die. To the degree that pain and fear can be lessened or removed from living and dying increases the opportunity for the living to live life to its fullest extent and for the dying to experience dying to its fullest extent. In both instances, transformative experiences.

I am neither dead nor dying other than in the sense that life itself is terminal. However, knowing that I, too, will die some day, any day for that matter, I have decided to share with my wife and children words to be read at my memorial service and instructions to be carried out upon my passing to lessen the burden on those I love of dealing with their loss and to ease my transition into the beyond.

I wish to die a natural death, not a modern death, the ending of my life prolonged by artificial means. If the next step for me to take to continue living is to be placed on life support, no way would I want to stay around under such circumstances. When the time comes for me to leave this existence, so be it. Of course, should the quality of my life be of a positive nature, my choice would be stay as long as possible with my loved ones. However, I might decide to end it all when the life I am called upon to live no longer offers me what I need and want to live life my way.

There are two life scenarios that would give me reason to seriously consider to not go on living. If Paula, the love of my life, were no longer here to share life's travails and joys with me, I would want my life to end. Also, God and Goddess forbid, if either Ana or Ben were to die before me, I would be very tempted to end my life. The pain permeating my entire being, heart, mind and soul, should either of my children pass on while I were still alive would be too much for me to bear.

My dear wife Paula and my dear children Ana Rebeca and Ben Rafael, I ask you to forgive me for all the angry moments I have shown you and to pardon me for whatever pain, despair and shame I have caused you. I ask you to cherish me for all the happy moments I have shared with you and to treasure whatever joy and pleasure, meaning and fulfillment I have brought to you. Know in the deepest realms of your hearts that I shall always love you, always be with you, and that we will meet again.

I hope and pray that your hearts will be able to express to me the love and compassion I have always felt from you; that you will always cherish the time we have had together; that I will never be alone; that I will always have your love; that you will tell me you do not want me to suffer any more; that you will let me go and give me permission to die.

Where and how do I wish to die? At home, or perhaps by the sea watching waves merging into ocean, or in a flower filled meadow under an endless blue sky watching a cloud come and go. At peace, with family, without undue pain or suffering, and in the arms of my loved ones. I would prefer not to leave the world kicking and screaming at my fate, but as if I were gliding into the universal and the eternal. Quite simply, I pray for a dying to be embraced.

Given the role that "food of the gods" has played in my life, opening up doors into the mystery of existence in ways that have enhanced my time on earth and made me aware that, at my essence, I am more than my body, I wish to die under the influence of marijuana. In fact, if there is truth to the belief that we die as we have lived, and being high with kindred souls has been among the fondest and most bonding experiences of my life, let all in attendance at my passing also be high on ganja. I cannot imagine what better way to depart, to make the transition from body to spirit, than with a little help from my stoked, stoned and euphoric loved ones.

Believing in the right to get high by means of smoking bud rather than drinking bud doesn't play very well these days.

Neither does the idea that getting high can be good for you, revealing a non-ordinary state of consciousness that is better suited for meeting many of the challenges to be encountered during our living and our dying than being in the state of consciousness called normal or straight. To be sure, marijuana, as is true for any other mind altering substance, legal or illegal, can be abused, made part of one's life in a careless or excessive fashion, without respect for its immense power, its potential to light the way to the deepest and highest levels of the human possibility. On the other hand, marijuana can also be used responsibly and respectfully, as a medium for navigating life's choppy and turbulent waters, as is often the case of dying with less fear, less pain and with greater acceptance.

Before I die I want a good traveling in heaven celebration, where those whose lives I touched during my lifetime would honor the life I have lived. The invitation to this event is to read as follows:

I've had my share of trials and tribulations. I've also had my fair share, in fact, more than I could have ever expected given my origins, of triumphs and joys. I have loved and been loved. My students have told me how much I affected their lives and continue to do so. I have been a worker in the fields of peace and justice, walking the talk that, after all is said and done, we are all brothers and sisters. I have been blessed by being immersed in earth journeys that have filled me with awe and the knowledge that I am part of a greater whole, that I am wave and ocean. I have had a good life. No, to tell the truth, I have had a great life.

And at the time of my dying, surrendering to life's outgoing tide, let it be in the presence of my loved ones who will give me permission to let go, and allow me to weep until I can shed no more tears for my heart will be broken. I will miss my Paula, my Ana, my Ben. Yes, I am on my way home, to where my life came forth. Yet, I am also leaving home, the one I made with my loved ones. One is not more mine than the other. To depart from either is a time of sadness. Yes, it is written in the cards that our destiny is to meet again. But all we truly have is this moment, whether it be when we are living or when we are dying. So, let us embrace each other as if this were our last moment to feel the warmth of each other's body, for, in truth, this is our last moment together. Hold me tightly and tell me you will always love me.

Cover my body with flower petals from my garden and release butterflies at my memorial service to remind all present of death as well as birth being transformative life experiences. Merging with the timeless and endless, I will cease to be. No longer wave. I am ocean. My death will end my life, but not my relationship with you. In your memories and hearts, I will remain alive.

Everything changes, everything passes. My party is about to be come to an end. The time is coming for me to go. So, if the spirit moves you, put on your dancing shoes and join Paula, Ana, Ben and I for a farewell celebration of my life. It is now my turn to be wished good traveling in heaven as we dance, dance, dance the day and night away. Send me off graced by bliss.

I shall also be most grateful, as was the case with my older brother, to have died after my mother's passing to spare her from having to hear those dreaded words once again: "Yetta, your son is dead." Burying two of her boys is more than enough to ask a mother to bear. I cannot imagine the immensity and depth of the scars inflicted on body, mind and soul to bear witness to the death of a child. My heart would ache to its core as I lay dying if I were to bear witness to my mother's heart aching at the passing of yet another son.

To be read at my memorial service by Ana with the sounds of Ben playing music of his choosing composed for either drums or guitar in the background:

> *The Golden God, the Self, the immortal Swan*
> *leaves the small nest of the body, goes where He wants.*
> *He moves through the realm of dreams; makes numberless*
> *forms; delights in sex; eats, drinks, laughs with His*
> *friends;*
> *But he is not attached to anything that He sees;*
> *and after He has wandered in the realms of dream and*
> *awakeness, has tasted pleasures and experienced*
> *good and evil,*
> *He returns to the blissful state from which He began.*
> *As a fish swims forward to one riverbank then the other,*
> *Self alternates between awakeness and dreaming.*
> *As an eagle, weary from long flight, folds its wings,*
> *gliding down to its nest, Self hurries to the realm*
> *of dreamless sleep, free of desires, fear, pain.*
> *As a man in sexual union with his beloved*
> *Is unaware of anything outside ort inside,*

so a man in union with Self knows nothing, wants nothing,
has found his heart's fulfillment and is free of sorrow.
Father disappears, mother disappears, gods
And scriptures disappear, thief disappears, murderer,
rich man, beggar disappear, world disappears,
good and evil disappear; he has passed beyond sorrow.
Self is everywhere, shining forth from all being,
Vaster than the vast, subtler than the most subtle,
Unreachable, yet nearer than breath, than heartbeat.
Eye cannot see it, ear cannot hear it nor tongue
utter it; only in deep absorption can the mind,
grown pure and silent, merge from the formless truth.
He who finds it is free; he has found himself;
he has solved the great riddle; his heart forever is at peace.
Whole, he enters the Whole, His personal Self
returns to its radiant, intimate, deathless source.
As rivers lose name and form when they disappear
into the sea, the sage leaves behind all traces
when he disappears into the light. Perceiving the truth,
he becomes truth; he passes beyond all suffering,
beyond death; all the knots of his heart are loosened.

                                 The Upanishads

    I, too, in the Silverstein family tradition wish to be purified by fire. I, too, wish to have my ashes cast into the Pacific Ocean, into Haleakala, into the roots of a newly planted tree both on Maui as well as in my backyard at home. Soul freed from embodied existence, resting sufficiently to gather the wherewithal and courage to return to the in-body experience, to face the challenge of once again having my heart to open here on earth. Why? To do what the gods and goddesses yearn for that they may be complete—incarnation in order to experience the fruits and ecstasy of earthly love.

Paula's and Louis's Story I

Taking a moment's respite from a long walk on a crystal clear fall day, my wife and I sat on a sidewalk in the East Village of New York City. Paula turned to me, held my hands in hers, looked into my eyes, and said, "Louis, my love, I want you to promise me something. Tell me you will not die." I responded, "To make such a promise is beyond my powers, but I will love you for as long as I live, and when I die, although no longer by your side in this world, know within your heart that I will never stop loving you"

Our tears turned to laughter. Is it not true that it takes both rain and sunshine to make a rainbow?

Paula went on to inform me of a saint who is coming to Maui, a woman who has lived in a cave for thirteen years meditating in pursuit of enlightenment. I replied, "Living in a cave for thirteen years is a piece of cake. Humans have been doing that since time immemorial. Tell me about those folks who reside in the realm of relationships for thirteen years, especially those brave souls raising children, and who remain relatively intact, whole, still loving, and you will be in the presence of a saint."

It is neither in thought nor isolation, but within the context of relationship that we come to know ourselves. Relationship is the mirror of our consciousness. This mirror will reveal who we truly are behind our makeup, no matter how skillfully put on—our fears, our loneliness, our aspirations, our ability to give and receive, our joys and our sorrows.

I know this because the road I have navigated into the arms of my Paula, my beloved soul mate, has been filled with love gained and lost more than once. Being in a cave on a mountain has been a relative piece of cake for me. Being married has taken me to heaven. It has also taken me to hell. Between the two being dead while alive has also made its presence known.

Relationships and love are among life's most treasured pursuits and gifts. At the same time, to pursue enduring love in a relationship is to embark on a life journey filled with disappointment, hurt and sorrow, often resulting in separation from self and others rather than union, which is a form of living death. I speak from experience, having loved and lost in the form of three marriages and divorces prior to finding the love of my life. Each time a love that once was a burning flame had turned to ashes, akin to a cremation. Not only was I left feeling as if life were not worth living, but that a basic part of me had died in the form of my heart having shut down. My heart, which is the source of passion in the human body, continued to fulfill its obligations and responsibilities in the process of keeping me alive, but in a feeble manner, sort of like being on life support rather than life energizing. I felt as if I had joined the walking dead.

Yet, everything changes. However long and bitter the dead of winter is, spring will surely follow with its accompaniment of life emerging from the shadows into the light. For me spring came into my life in the form of Paula. There I was, performing on stage at a faculty talent show, and, as she would tell me later, her eyes, as if they had a life of their own, sought mine out, attracted by a beam of light shining from them.

She went on to say, "I became spellbound. I could not move my feet. I said to myself, 'holy shit, I'm in trouble. How am I going to get out of this mess?' Luckily, I was standing next to the table where the food for the evening had been placed. You walked over, began eating a yogurt, seemingly paying no attention to me. However, after a few moments had passed, you turned your body toward me and asked, 'Would you like to go out to dinner with me?' I replied, 'Yes,' and then my feet became unglued and I could walk."

Why, still feeling so down and withdrawn, did I reach out to Paula? To be completely honest, I really do not know. Perhaps because, as I have often thought, we are actors and actresses in a play already written, acting out a script that we cannot see, but which moves us in one life direction or another. All I know is that evening was the first step of my being "reborn" into life's passions, and a life without passion is to be existing in a prison, a tomb if you will, without bars, but nonetheless still a prison.

Closing my eyes, I envision myself sitting beside a pond with water lilies and blue green algae floating on its surface. I ask for help to make it through life's journey, and she takes my hand. I weep, and she comes to my side. I listen for singing, and she fills my ears with the lilting sounds of her voice. I pine for love, and she takes me within her. I wish to return to the body in which I was born, and she leads me beyond time into eternity. Her lips speak words that I have always wanted to hear from a wife, "Promise me that we shall meet again."

Paula, my dear wife, gentle and beautiful creature that you are, I love you so much that it takes all my courage to be with you. How dare you enter into the deepest recesses of my being, your presence enticing me out of inner closets where I have always hidden from intimacy? Am I to be slain, burned by the heat and warmth of your love, my death throes being a call to my higher self to rise up from the ashes of my defenses?

In a dream Paula, Ana and Ben encircle me as they chant "asat chit ananda" (eternal bliss consciousness) over and over again so that no sounds of the universe but theirs are to be heard. Slowly, each of my loved ones, in turn, approaches, sits down as close to me as possible, holds my hands, touches their lips to mine, and very consciously and deliberately breathes love into my open and receptive mouth.

My body armor breaks up into small pieces as it crumbles about me. Walls come tumbling down, and a bridge appears above the moat of separation from others that has been my companion since childhood, allowing those who love me to cross over into my life. Kundalini energy moves up my outstretched spine into my brain as I glide into ecstasy.

Turning my attention to Paula, her words reach out to me. "I had hoped to accomplish more in this lifetime, but I am not going to complain. I've had a great life. We were able to get together again, to have a family, to have fun. I love you and I know that you love me."

Once again, facing the impermanence of our existence has resulted in our taking the time to inhale life's flowers, of which love can be among the most fragrant and long lasting; to say to each other words that transcend time and space. Should my epitaph simply state, "I loved and was loved," I would die a wealthy, fulfilled and happy man.

To create such an epitaph and have it speak truth, there was work to be undertaken on my part based on the realization that being a lover is not enough. I needed to nourish the object of my love. I needed to realize that the woman to whom I was wed has taken my suffering as her suffering, my happiness as her happiness, my life and death as her life and death. I needed to let go of my life as lover in bed as the sole definition of what it meant to love a woman in order to create a relationship reality of such a nature that my wife would experience the daily sunny warmth of happiness as well as the wildest reaches of joy that I bear unto her.

I had grown into the realization that if I did not live my life in accordance with a credo of love, devotion and surrender in relation to Paula, when the time of dying came for either of us, I would never be able to stop crying, because I did not practice how to be truly happy with the love of my life. The tears would flow endlessly because not having been filled up with life, I would feel empty, desiring that which I could no longer have.

Paula's and Louis's Story II

Lying in bed, we share our thoughts and feelings about dying and death. Not in a theoretical sense, for we are no longer young and the death of many who were part of our lives has served to remind us that we, too, are mortal. It is our demise, not that of others, we are discussing.

"It makes me so sad to think that you will no longer be with me. I just want to cry. Louis, as close as humanely possible to the time that we will part in this lifetime, I want you to kiss me. I want to feel your breath enter my mouth and flow into every cell of my body. I want you inside of me. I want you deeply inside of me. I want to feel you explode inside of me. After you are gone, I not only want to have you as thoughts in my mind and feelings in my heart, I also want to touch you, to have you in my body as a felt presence. And when both of us have passed, I want some of our ashes to be mixed together and placed in a grave so that we are united in the afterlife as we were in this life. Let all who visit our graveside know our love and desire to be together stood the test of time."

During the night, I have a dream. On dark green fields of eternity, I kiss Paula's lips as she drinks fragrant sweet nectar from my mouth. From her lips words are spoken that are seared into my memory. "We have known each other a thousand times and still you love me." I have loved and been loved by Paula all my life. And that is how I want my life to end. Even before we met in person, I now know that her love was always there calling out to me, albeit at times in a soft whisper, serving as both beacon and guide to sustain me in my life's journey to find her.

As a child, in the second grade, I was infatuated with a classmate, drawn to her for reasons unknown to me. I say this because to gaze at her with a desire to be close to her, to touch her, was to transgress an unspoken, but nonetheless rigidly enforced cultural norm, and I was a "good" and obedient child. Whites and blacks did not mix in such a manner, at least not during the light of day. And, if that reality was not enough to cause alarm, she was not of my faith.

I believe she was mostly unaware of what was going on in my mind and heart, because an occasional "Hi" was the extent to which we had any kind of interchange other than the one day our eyes met and a warm smile broke out on each of our faces. Yet, memories of my fascination with her stayed with me as the years of my life have gone by.

When Paula and I decided to get married, it was our wish to be joined together as husband and wife within a sacred setting and our union blessed by a holy person. The fact that we were "outlaws" of a sort, she being Catholic and a woman of color from the Bronx via Puerto Rico and I being Jewish and from Brooklyn, probably had something to do with a desire for our marriage to be officially sanctified.

However, the catholic priest said no unless I converted. The rabbi said no unless she converted. The Zen Buddhist asked us if we loved each other? We said yes. He, in turn, said yes. Why, we asked, telling him about the catholic priest and the rabbi? "Because, you are in love, and wherever there is love, holiness is present. By marrying you I am simply giving witness to what already exists—a place of worship called the union of Paula and Louis."

Ana's Story

A month or so prior to my daughter Ana's third birthday, she either fell or jumped out of the crib she was resting in, her head hitting the floor with a loud thump. Luckily, one of our neighbors was a nurse who, upon giving Ana a thorough look over, said she seemed to be fine, but advised us to keep an eye on her. Should Ana become dizzy, or if any fluid were to come out of her ears or mouth, these were signs indicating she needed immediate medical attention. The day passed, and Ana appeared to be her normal self with no discernible aftereffects from her head's encounter with the floor.

All seemed to be well with Ana the next morning, but for reasons unknown, I had a strong feeling she needed to be taken to the hospital in order to be examined by a physician. Paula asked me why I believed this was necessary? All I could say in response was that I needed to trust my feelings.

Arriving at Chicago's Children's Memorial Hospital's emergency room, we were asked the usual questions. What was wrong? When did the accident occur? Did she lose consciousness? Was she bleeding at any time? And, of course, is Ana insured? Upon completing the necessary forms, we waited until we could be seen by one of the overworked physicians on duty. After examining Ana, he ordered that x-rays be taken of her head. Ana was whisked away to the radiation department while I waited for her in the examination cubicle. Nearly a half hour later, Ana was brought back and we were told that the attending physician would be with us shortly.

He informed me that Ana had fractured her skull, but there was no need to be concerned. Young children's skulls are still relatively soft, in fact not even completely closed, and fractures of the kind that Ana had suffered would, in all likelihood, cause no permanent damage, healing on their own without any further medical intervention necessary. All I need do was to keep a close eye on her, and should she, as the nurse had also advised, experience dizziness or fluid leakage from an orifice, we were to seek immediate medical attention.

Feeling great relief, Ana and I took the elevator to the main waiting room where we could rest for a few moments and obtain some snack food. After a few minutes had gone by, a doctor entered the room, walked over to us holding Ana's x-rays, sat down next to me, and proceeded to tell me that she had examined the x-rays and, for reasons she was not sure of, recommended that Ana have a MRI. When I asked why she had looked at Ana's x-rays in the first place, she responded that she didn't know why, but that a strong feeling on her part made her do so.

Off Ana went for her MRI. Upon being informed of the results, the world as I had known it fell apart. For a moment or two, it felt like the life force had been sucked out of me. Her MRI clearly showed a cyst present in the middle of her brain requiring immediate medical attention. No, no, no . . . this cannot be so was the thought that flooded my brain. She seemed fine, in good spirits, bouncy and buoyant as always. For reasons of maintaining my sanity, I asked, "Could there be an error, the MRI having been read incorrectly?" In reply, I received a simple and straightforward, but nonetheless devastating answer. "No."

Somewhat shell shocked to put it mildly, I called my wife to inform her of the news. "Oh, my god!" she cried out, followed by a piercing cry, her sobbing filled my ears and flooded my heart. I told Paula that she needed to compose herself, and to take a taxi to the hospital to be with Ana and to participate in a conference with the doctors to discuss where do we go from here?

The primary outcome of the meeting was a decision on our part to avail ourselves of the expertise of a neurologist and follow his recommendations. Having much faith and trust in our family physician who had also helped deliver Ana, Paula called Dr. Ettner in order to inform him of Ana's condition and to obtain a referral. As fate would have it, he had studied with one of the country's most prominent neurologists, Dr. Huttenlocher, who was in residence at Wyler's Children Hospital, which is affiliated with the University of Chicago in Hyde Park. He strongly advised us to have Dr. Huttenlocher see Ana and that we were to follow his recommendations.

After viewing Ana's MRI and examining her, Dr. Huttenlocher informed us that the cyst did not appear to be cancerous, but was of the kind known as arachnoid. Arachnoid cysts are fluid filled sacs that occur in arachnoid membranes that cover the brain, and can either be symptomatic, headaches, seizures and abnormal accumulation of excessive cerebrospinal fluid in the brain (hydrocephalus), or asymptomatic in nature as was the case with Ana. However, he went to say that given its size and location in Ana's brain, she would in all likelihood suffer from its effects in the future, and that she should either be shunted in order to have it drained periodically, or have the cyst surgically removed.

Why do bad things happen to good people, especially children? Paula and I realized we had neither time nor energy to devote to this perennial question. Life had taught us in so many ways that crap happens, and that you either attend to the mess or let it spread and envelop you. All we knew is that our focus needed to be on what was best for Ana and how to bring that about. We did not want Ana to suffer or walk with the sword of Damocles hanging over her head. Our desire was that Ana, our child, be given every opportunity not only to live out her life, but to do so in possession of all her faculties.

Dr. Huttenlocher, in turn, referred us to Dr. Dohrmann, a neurosurgeon who he believed was best qualified to perform the kind of surgery Ana needed. Off we went to the Playboy Building where his office was located. An office completely decorated in black, including walls and furniture and framed photographs of beautiful women fell somewhat outside of what we would have expected for a medical office. However, we were in pursuit of skills not lifestyle, so we waited patiently to be ushered into his office.

Dr. Dohrmann agreed with Dr. Huttenlocher's diagnosis of Ana's condition and the options available to us. Shunting would carry less risk, but the problem with choosing this procedure was that the shunts often become infected and have to be replaced, which would require Ana's having to undergo the trauma of being operated on a number of times during her lifetime. Additionally, we had been told if anything were to go wrong during the surgical procedure, resulting in damage to the patient, it was the anesthesia, not the procedure, most likely to be at fault. Although the odds of such a mishap occurring were low, they do happen. Obviously, the more times spent in the operating room, the greater the likelihood of an accident of such a nature taking place.

However, should we opt for surgical removal of the cyst, Dr. Dohrmann informed us that if anything were to go wrong, at best Ana might be permanently brain damaged. The worst-case scenario was that she wouldn't make it out of the operating room. Furthermore, due to where in her brain the cyst was found to be, an experimental procedure utilizing ultrasound to determine its exact location would be required in order to puncture it, allowing the fluid contained within to drain off. He went on to assure us that he was among the most experienced surgeons in the country who were utilizing ultrasound to guide forays into the brain, and he felt confident the operation would be performed successfully.

Paula and I left his office feeling both deathly frightened and overwhelmed with the responsibility cast upon us to decide our daughter's fate. Shunting would be safer in the short run, but we did not like it at all that Ana might have to undergo repeated operations with their attendant risks during the course of her lifetime. Surgery was likely to have the most positive long-term effects, but the risks involved in going that route were almost too much for us to deal with.

What do you do when you do not know what to do and reason is not to be the guiding factor in arriving at a decision? Yes, remaining objective in critical life situations make sense so that we can be clear-headed in the decision-making process. However, what we were dealing with did not lend itself to the seeming efficiency of a cost-benefit analysis.

Paula and I turned to prayer, input from the world of spiritual advisors whom we had known for years as well as the advice of friends and family, and also read everything we could find on the subject. Yet, in the final analysis, it was our intuition, just somehow knowing directly and instinctively and trusting an innate part of ourselves, which had always served us so well in the past, that proved to be the deciding factor in opting for the surgery.

Off we went to the hospital to settle Ana in and prepare her for the surgery. All appeared to be going smoothly, whatever that means when your child is about to undergo a brain procedure, until hair, yes hair, and the feelings associated with it demanded its role in our life drama. When a nurse informed Ana that her head would have to be shaved in order to perform the surgery, her response was an emphatic "No! No! No!" "Amidst tears and a shaking body, she screamed, "I want my hair. No operation."

Without the removal of Ana's hair, the surgery could not proceed, and using force to remove her hair was an action that neither Paula nor I were willing to give our consent to. We felt Ana had already been traumatized, that the surgery would also prove to be traumatic, and that overriding her strong feelings about and objections to her hair being removed, which in her eyes had to be seen as a violation of her persona, was asking too much of Ana. There had to be another way out of this dilemma.

We conferred with the nurse who suggested that we ask the hospital's resident play therapist to intervene, a suggestion that proved to be both a lifesaver and a heart mender. The therapist, in reality a maker of magic, invited Ana to go with her to the playroom where she would meet other children and where she could play with numerous toys and dolls.

In a most skillful manner, the therapist encouraged Ana to make friends with a doll that not only looked like her, but also possessed a head of hair, black, long, flowing, very similar to Ana's. After Ana and the doll became very attached to each other, which occurred over a course of two days, the therapist told Ana that her new friend was ill, requiring brain surgery, but Betsy, the name Ana had given to the doll, was unwilling to undergo the surgery because her head had to be shaved for the operation to proceed.

The therapist went on to tell Ana that without the surgery, Betsy would always not be well and that she might even worsen. She then asked, "Ana, would you be willing to talk to your new friend and try to convince her to willing to have the surgery?" Without a moment's hesitation, Ana said "Yes."

Walking to a corner of the room with the doll in her arms, Ana engaged Betsy in what appeared to be from where my wife and I were standing a very spirited and emotional conversation. When the discussion was over, Ana informed the therapist that she had told Betsy how important it was for her to have the operation, that even without her hair she would still be beautiful, that her hair would soon grow back, and that no matter how she looked Ana would always love her. And miracle upon miracle, Ana also told the therapist of her readiness to undergo her own surgery.

After Paula, Gloria, Ana's grandmother and I had been waiting, hoping and praying for close to three hours wondering how the surgery was proceeding, Dr. Dohrmann exited the operating room to inform us that so far so good, but it would be another four or five hours until he would know for certain if all had gone as planned. Time can be a racehorse or a snail. Notwithstanding our desire to whip the hands of the clock on the wall so that time would move along at the pace we wanted, the seconds, minutes went by ever so slowly, very much out of sync with our racing thoughts and emotions. How long is eternity? For the three of us it would last however long it took until we knew if we had our Ana back and in what condition.

The doors to the operating room opened and Dr. Dohrmann approached us, the look on his face revealed nothing about what we were about to hear. Joyous words entered our ears, caressed our minds and hearts and lifted our spirits to the highest realm of heaven. "The surgery was successful. Ana is doing fine. Ana is lucky. Although she was asymptomatic, when we pierced the cyst, the fluid within it splattered all over the room. Obviously the cyst was under such pressure, it was going to burst. Just imagine what would have happened inside her brain had we not operated when we did. She is resting comfortably now in the recovery room where Ana can be closely monitored. After that, she will be taken back to her hospital room where you can see her."

As we patiently waited, Paula and I gave thought to what the surgeon had told us. No symptoms on her part, but Ana's surgery was not only absolutely necessary, it had to be done now. Did our daughter fall out of the crib, a fortuitous occurrence to say the least? Or, had Ana, impelled by her guardian angel for want of knowing how else to get us to pay attention to the mysterious forces often at work in our lives, jumped for reasons, perhaps, even unknown to her at the time?

Ana's life had been spared. The loss of a child is one of life's greatest tragedies, a wound that time often cannot mend, a blow to heart, mind and spirit often incapable of being healed. My wife and I had come close to knowing if this were indeed a fact of life, having been spared from having to deal with the absolute horror of such a truth by virtue of good fortune, a skillful play therapist, the sure and steady hands of a master surgeon, and the strong life force within our daughter.

A happy ending, but at the same time, in Paula's and my mind our belief in life making sense had been shattered. An angel sent to us from heaven had been dealt a heavy blow of such a nature as to jeopardize her life. Still a child, yet having to confront her mortality, this is not what we had in mind when my wife and I envisioned our daughter's life journey. Giving thought to and having death and dying was for the likes of us, not for those of a tender age, or so we had thought.

Ana's & Ben's Story

It is evening. Paula and I are lying in bed sharing our experiences and thoughts of the day. Paula tells me that Ana voiced a desire to learn more about the two of us before we die. Mother and father look at each other with our eyes wide open feeling in our guts the extent to which the words "before we die" stir up heart rendering emotions within us. On another occasion such words would bring tears to our eyes, for who, in his or her right mind, would want the love we have known as husband and wife as well as parents to our children to end. Yes, there is the unending love of souls, but being embraced lovingly by your lover or your children in the here and now, to feel the warmth of their bodies against your own, matches anything eternal.

Ana, who has said time and time again that she can't imagine living without us, for her to begin accepting the reality that mom and dad will not always be around, albeit frightening, is a necessary realization and a big step in the process of her taking flight and making her own nest, to becoming her own person. On the other hand, Ben has always been of a different nature, telling us he will, of course, be sad when we die, but that will not mean that he should not or would not go on with his own life. Two children from the same womb, composed of egg and sperm from the identical two individuals, yet each their own person, possessed of a life script to be lived out in a manner necessary for coping with loss as well as to live in the present unfettered by life's necessary sorrows.

Our individual lives have a beginning and an end only in the sense that a chapter in a book has a beginning and an end. However, a chapter does not make a book any more than an individual life is the totality of a family's journey. My life did not begin with me but with the flesh and blood that came from Jack and Yetta. My life will continue on beyond my death in the children who were made from the blood and flesh of Paula and I. Yes, a body ends, but not a life. All that which makes up and flows through my body existed before the I known as Louis came into being, and will continue on in another configuration after I cease to exist in my present form.

Once, while standing before a thousand year old Redwood tree of towering dimensions, in my imagination I saw the sapling it once was as well as its decayed remnants once it dies, which, in turn, will feed other trees, and in the process of doing so become an integral part of them. Once we arrive at the realization that all of existence is interconnected, that there is neither beginning nor end to a life, we are offered the opportunity to live our lives freed from the anxiety attached to feelings of separateness.

Paula's and Gloria's Story

In 2006, sixty years after Paula came into this world, she and I flew to Miami, Florida to be with her mother on the occasion of Gloria's ninety-second birthday. Gloria, usually more there in another realm than here, from the day of Paula's birth, had always found fault with her daughter's physical appearance.

Paula, a woman of color, was the dark child, very different in appearance from her mother's two other children. Gloria, as the years passed up to the present moment, had continually asked Paula the same question. "Where did you come from?" She was never satisfied with her daughter's answer. "From you mom."

Gloria stared at Paula as if she had never seen her daughter in quite the same way as she is taking her in at this very moment. Words of gold were spoken by mother to daughter. "You are so beautiful." Gloria closes her eyes and drifts off into sleep.

Paula, her eyes filled with tears, turned towards me and said, "Finally, after all these years, my mother recognizes me for who I am, the child she brought into this world through her body. I am HER child. Gloria has always accepted my soul. Now she has finally accepted my body."

Gloria's Story

Once again Paula and I have returned to Miami to be with Gloria on the occasion of her birthday. This time around it's her ninety-fourth.

As she is doing at this very moment and most moments of her life when she is not resting or sleeping in bed, Gloria is sitting on a couch, her somewhat frail body seemingly too worn down to do much standing up. However, her body is moving in place, not large movements but ones discernable enough to show that she is taking in the rhythm of the mariachi band hired to celebrate Gloria's day of birth. What better way to pay due honor and respect to a life well and fully lived than with music, which at its very essence, is a celebration of life as well as the voices of gods and goddesses reminding us that we are not alone.

Sounds of horns, accordion and voice fill the room, entering our ears as the pathway to our souls. Gloria is moving even more distinctly to the beat. Perhaps, she is recalling her nights spent at the Roseland Ballroom in Manhattan, when her body flew across the dance floor to the music of Tito Puente, Mongo Santamaria, Celia Cruz and other Latin stars. Paula would often tell me, "What a dancer my mother was. She loved, absolutely loved to dance."

Maria, Gloria's other daughter, is beckoning to her to stand up and dance. Gloria is moving her head from side to side indicating a no because she knows she can't. In order not to deny Gloria the pleasure of feeling the warm body of her daughter next to hers, Maria insists that her mother get up off the couch and join her on what is passing for a dance floor today. Finally, Gloria relents. With a broad smile on her face, Gloria embraces Maria as their feet slowly move in place in tune with the music being played.

At this very moment in time, Gloria has forgotten who she is. An old woman whose primary movements consist of being assisted to the dining room table, the bathroom and her bedroom. For a minute or two, Gloria is living in the present, her thoughts and feelings focused neither on the past nor on the future. "Yes, once I could dance. Yes, I am going to die, but I am very happy." Her joy is boundless. The power of music to bring life into our lives, to get us into the now, this very moment, is indeed a blessing.

The music comes to an end. The mariachi band has to leave. Gloria has returned to sitting on the couch. Without a word being spoken, the smile on her face says it all. "I am so happy."

Mike's Story

A gathering of the Columbia tribe is taking place at Chicago's Millennium Greek Restaurant to celebrate the memory of Mike Alexandroff, former President of Columbia College Chicago, who passed on just a few short weeks ago. However, his spirit lives on. In each and every colleague's face, I see Mike's presence, for his vision of Columbia is embedded in their life work as educators.

Our journey began in the 1960's during "the times, they are changing." Assembled by Mike into his educational dream team, those of us who would come to be known as the "long marchers," a phrase with ties to those who marched a very long distance with Mao Tze Tung in order to get to a place where they could regroup their forces, before continuing on the battle to liberate China, were given the charge and freedom to change, be it through means of reform or revolution, the world of higher education by creating a new kind of educational experience for those wanting to study in the fields of arts and communication media oriented towards being able to make, at the very least, a living wage after receiving a Columbia College degree.

Let us go back to rented space in storefronts and churches in various locations on the north side of Chicago as well to a few floors of a dilapidated warehouse building on Ohio and Lake Shore Drive. We were a handful of brilliant, visionary, iconoclastic, dedicated and disciplined collection of musicians, dancers, photographers, graphic designers, filmmakers, actors/actresses, writers, television and radio specialists, journalists, social scientists, historians and humanists, joined together to bring into being Columbia College Chicago.

An arts based higher education institution that would hold its doors wide open, extending an invitation to "your tired, your poor, your huddled masses yearning to breathe free," requiring of each not past success, but the potential and drive to be all that they can be. A four year urban, open-admissions college centered on teaching as contrasted to publishing, on the creative as well the critical, on learning by doing from whose who do what they teach, giving equal weight to process (the art of teaching) as well as to subject matter. Columbia was poor in terms of material wealth, but rich in talent and vision, in possession of a dream that could not denied.

It didn't take long for me to realize that working at Columbia was akin to joining an extended family. I remember receiving a telephone call from Mike shortly after he had heard that my daughter Ana required major brain surgery. He told me to do whatever was necessary to best serve my daughter's interests, not to spare any expense in getting her the best the medical care the world had to offer, and that he and Columbia would stand behind me financially whatever the cost.

Of course, at Columbia there were also the good times. I recall fondly the occasions when, during my tenure as Dean of the College, Mike would call me in order to inquire as to which of my dean's duties I was attending to at the moment? No matter what I said, his response always remained the same. "A more urgent task is at hand. The Cubs are playing San Francisco." Off we went to Wrigley Field. Mike knew that all work and no play makes for a sad and dispirited administrator, which would be reflected in the workings of the college.

Mike truly loved baseball, his dream job being not as a college president, but as the baseball commissioner. This being so, on the occasion of his fiftieth birthday, I contacted Thaine Lyman, Chair of our Television Department as well as one of the chief honchos in the technical area at channel 9, WGN-TV, the Chicago station that telecasted the Cub games. I asked him if he would be willing to use his connections to see what could be arranged to present Mike with a surprise gift he would carry to the grave with him? Thaine replied that he would give it a good try.

Thaine turned to Harry Carey, who did the play-by-play broadcast for WGN—at the Cub games, and lo and behold, magic was set into action. A few weeks later, just after Mike's birthday, according to pre-arranged plans, Mike joined Thaine for dinner at a local restaurant. Picture this. Mike is sitting at his table waiting for Thaine to show up. Who comes into the dining room? None other than one of Mike's foremost idols. No, not Naom Chomsky, albeit held in high esteem by Mike, but Willie Mays, the all-star center fielder for the San Francisco Giants. Mays looks around, recognizes Mike due to his having been cued in as to what he looked like and where he would be sitting, walks over to Mike's table, introduces himself, and asks Mike if he could join him for dinner? If ever yes was the only answer to a question, this was the occasion for it. The "Say Hey Kid" and Mike hit it off like crazy, and a wonderful and memorable, absolutely unforgettable, evening unfolded.

Well, Mike is in heaven now. He's back together with virtually all of the other long-marchers I came to know during my long career at Columbia College Chicago. Jane, his wife. Thaine Lyman, aforementioned Television Department Chair. Al Weisman, Public Relations Department Chair. Bob Edmonds, Film Department Chair. Harry Bouras, Humanities faculty member. Daryl Feldmeir, Journalism Department Chair.

Bill Russo Music Department Chair. Ed Morris, Television Department Chair. Herb Pinzke, Graphic Arts faculty. Brian Katz, Photography faculty. Hubert Davis, Dean of Student Services. John Scheibel, Chief Financial Officer. Jake Caref, Building & Grounds. Sam Baskin, Board of Trustees. Bud Salk, Board of Trustees and History faculty. Dwight Follett, Chair of the Board of Trustees.

And with Mike being in heaven, we know one thing for certain. Heaven is going to be affordable, open admissions and deal with practical matters of the soul.

Some of the most beautiful human interactions that I have witnessed have occurred between dying patients and supportive families and friends. Sometimes the quality of human interactions in the terminal phase far exceeds anything the patient or family has experienced in life.

Physician (Anonymous)

Jake's Story

Who was Jake? Not my father, but a dear friend and colleague, Columbia College's resident master carpenter and jack of all trades for many years. When told by his doctor that there was nothing left for the medical profession to do, and that he needed to accept the fact of his imminent death, in response

Jake quietly sang these words: "The party's over. It's time to call it a day. Take off your makeup. It's time to break up. The party's over." He then turned to the doctor, telling him what a good and beautiful man he was, which resulted in, not Jake, the dying, but the doctor, the living, shedding tears.

However, the beautiful and the not so beautiful often go hand-in-hand. And so the drama unfolded. Jake wanted his children, all mature adults in their fifties, to undergo DNA testing to prove that they were, indeed, his children. Why? Because he believed that his first wife, their mother, had been unfaithful and that her lover had fathered the children. Needless to say, his sons and daughter were outraged at this demand, refusing to comply, culminating in angry verbal exchanges between Jake and them. To be sure, not the ideal way for a family to deal with the final days of a life.

At Jake's urging I was called in by the family to help resolve this dispute. To cut to the quick, I asked the children to join me in the hallway to discuss what was transpiring between them and their father. They repeated their adamant opposition to undergoing the testing, which they believed was insulting and just another instance of their father's dictatorial ways. At the same time, they felt guilty over the state of affairs, not wanting the last days of Jake's life to be one of alienation from his children. Feeling trapped, they wanted some advice from me as to what could be done to resolve this contentious matter.

"What final gift did you want to leave with your father as his time was coming to an end? Is it one of rancor, of bitterness, of someone winning or losing an argument, of being right, at the cost of a soul departing ands souls left behind in a state of hurt and pain? It matters little to bring flowers to the dead. Jake will neither need nor appreciate them then. Bring flowers to him while he is still alive. Given where he and you are at this time in your lives, the flowers need to be those of forgiveness and love. Are you willing to let go of that which separates your from your father, and be man and woman enough to focus on his needs, because that is what is called for now? Otherwise, when he is gone, you will be left with feelings of guilt for the rest of your lives."

I realized I was asking a great deal of them, because many of our deepest attachments are to the emotions that bring us the most pain—hate, resentment, fear, anger and vengeance. There is a part of ourselves that believes it is essential never to forget or forgive anyone who has hurt us deeply. However, to not ask of others to go deep within themselves in order to tap into a higher sense of self is to do a disservice to our brother and sister travelers on planet earth. We are here to help others to grow, to be all they can be, not in the service of bringing death to others by means of arms that hurt and destroy, but in the service of arms that embrace others with love and compassion in our hearts.

"Go back into Jake's room. Say nothing. Just sit on his bed, hold his hands with compassion, stroke his back and forehead with gentleness, look into his eyes with love, and let him have his say. After he has finished venting his emotions, the anger in need of being released having gone its way, he will be open to hearing what you have to say to him, if it is of a healing nature. At that time, just tell him you love him, but these words must be sincere and come from a forgiving and loving heart."

After giving thought to what I had asked them to consider doing, Jake's sons and daughter went into the room, followed my words of advice, and all enfolded as I thought it would. Jake vented his anger, and when spent, lay back on his bed, and waited for their response. All was quiet, save for children telling their father, "I love you." As stillness filled the room, Jake fell asleep.

The next day, Jake passed.

Les's Story

On the occasion of a memorial service being held for a long-time colleague and friend, and at the request of his widow who asked that I share with those in attendance my thoughts about her husband in his capacity as a teacher, I composed and read the following eulogy, which, I was told by many present, is a testimonial not only to an individual's teaching career, but to the teaching profession itself.

> *To Les, dear colleague and friend,*
>
> *Hello, my name is Louis Silverstein. Les was my colleague at . . . No, that's not correct. Les remains my colleague at Columbia College Chicago. I say this because although a passing ends a life, it does not end a relationship, and those of us who were graced to have Les come into our lives know that the memories of what we shared and his spirit are still with us to carry forward into our lives.*

A few days ago, Priscilla called and asked me how I first met Les? I told her I could not recall. However, last night the aroma of my wife's chocolate chip cookies baking in the oven reminded me of our first meeting. Another of our colleagues at Columbia told me of a faculty member in the Journalism Department who made the damn best muffins in the world, and that I should obtain some from him to share with my peers during my department's next meeting.

I gave Les a call, ordered some muffins, and arranged a time and place to pick them up. As soon as we met, there was no question in my mind that I had come upon a kindred spirit. For what came with the muffins was a joyous presence, a broad and engaging smile, twinkling eyes, and a handshake filled with the flow of life. In essence, a Les that we all knew and will remember.

Les was a special teacher, respected and revered by his students, because he knew they were special people and treated them as such. Believing that his role was to teach students how to live, not just to make a living, and capable of reaching out beyond race, class, societal, family, cultural and self-imposed limitations to be all that they could be, if they were willing to discipline themselves to keep their eyes on the prize and to do the necessary hard work required to develop their talents and promise. For those who chose to do so, and their numbers are many, they were comforted by the fact that Les would be there to be leaned on if a little help from a friend intertwined with the transformative force of love were needed for them to get by and bloom.

As in the case of all great teachers, Les knew by virtue of his own life experiences that within each of his students there existed a seed, a magnificent seed, waiting to sprout and realize its full potential, and that his role as a teacher and mentor was to furnish his students with what it takes—mind body and soul, in the words of Columbia's mission statement, 'to author the culture of their times.'

Les was, in fact, the keeper of a dream for his students. For, when all was said and done, he taught them not just how to make a living but how to make a life. Yes, he knew that a mind is a terrible thing to waste, but so is a heart capable of loving and hands capable of embracing others to let them know you believe in them, care for them, and you are there for them.

Yes, Les travel into the light knowing that we at Columbia are most grateful for all your contributions to our community, that you made a difference in our lives, and that you not only were loved but are loved.

Bon voyage.

Ben's and Beatrice's Story

The telephone rings. I pick it up. "Hello, it's Beatrice." Without her saying another word, from the sound of her voice I know she is going to tell me that Ben, her beloved husband, has died.

Indeed, she informs me of Ben's passing two days ago, filling me on the details of the funeral service and burial.

Having met when she was fifteen and he a few years older, and being husband and wife for sixty-four years, until now their love had never waned, becoming just glowing embers serving as a reminder of what had once been a fire. To the contrary, the love they felt for each other had always remained a bright shining flame, their caring and compassionate way with each other was a joy to behold.

I put my wife Paula on the telephone so that she and Beatrice can talk. She tells Paula, "I've been crying for two days. I've known him all my life. And that still wasn't long enough."

Two days later, Paula and I are in a church on the far south side of Chicago paying our respects at Ben's memorial service. We are told that they were married in 1941, the beginning of a marriage that would last for sixty-four years. Due to a reason related to him being in the armed forces at the time, a civil ceremony was all that they could muster up for a wedding service. However, being the religious folk that they were, he promised Beatrice that the day would come when a minister of their faith would marry them in the eyes of God.

Two years ago, shortly before Ben became seriously ill, he asked Beatrice if she would marry him once again, that is, renew their vows? However, this time the senior minister of their church would conduct the service Beatrice, thrilled to the core at the prospect, answered, "Yes, I will"

Ben took his marriage ring with him. Why, because it symbolized a circle, and a circle has neither beginning nor end, and as such characterized the love he had always felt for his beloved Beatrice. In his eyes, their love was eternal, never to end. He believed in the deepest layers of his heart that when the time came for Beatrice's life on earth to come to an end, she would hear her him calling out her name, and they would be joined together again for eternity.

Beatrice's answer to Ben's entreaty to be with him throughout eternity had been answered many years before when she told him, "Yes, I will." "Till death do us part" is not recognized by eternity. The eternal does not begin with a death. It always exists. We are as much in it when we are alive as we are after we die.

Iwona's Story

Iwona, a former student of mine from almost twenty years ago who I have kept in contact with, was the guest presenter one summer in my "Death & Dying" class. She shared with the class the experience of returning to Poland to be with her mother in the home she had grown up in during the last month of her mother's life. Being a freelance photographer coupled with English being her second language, Iwona's customary mode of communication with an audience is to allow her images to speak for her. This being so, Iwona chose to write out and read rather than speaking extemporaneously what she wished to share with my students, to be followed by a question and answer period.

In her darkest hours, she was dressed in light. Maybe it was the divine light. The days of August and early September 2005 were bright and sunny, and the light that reached her was always soft. I remember the beauty of her silver hair . . . Her bed was facing the window with an open sky and a birch tree to the left. She loved birch trees and my brother always joked that he planted it for her.

I watched her acceptance and courage. She wanted to be herself, telling us that life is good, that it is time for her to go. She also wanted to leave us with a piece of advice: 'If you feel anger or resentment toward someone, write it on sand. The wind will know what to do with it. If someone does something good for you, write it in stone.'

She took morphine for a few days and said she didn't know whom she was. So she decided no morphine, drugs or feeding through tubes. And the long night came with no sleep. Mother had been cleansing herself all night long. My sister and I changed her diaper and bedding. Tired was her body. She was very weak. She was not eating and could only drink a sip or two of water.

I was supposed to bake a cake for a family gathering today. However, rather than doing that, I went upstairs to rest, but found myself thinking about mother and what the doctor had said this afternoon to the effect that it won't be long.

I came down, found my sister and her two daughters in the kitchen. I sat down by mother's bed and asked her if she needed anything? I watered her lips, and she reached for my hand, a gesture that alerted my senses. She was holding my hand tightly. Her body had little strength.

My sister accompanied by her daughters entered the room. The melodies of our voices speaking the words of 'Hail Mary' were connecting us in the hour of our mother's death. We could see her lips moving, but no sound came from her. The tenderness of her full awareness with her eyes focused beyond our reach was like a sign of her connecting with someone very dear to her.

'Can you see us mom? Can you see us mom?' my sister kept asking. Her head moved from left to right letting us know that we were no longer visible to her. She kept walking with her eyes further away from our reach.

'Can you hear us mom?' my sister asked. She kept on trying until our mother nodded her head, so clear was her yes.

She was leaving us and we were letting her go.

What happened after that was pure life taking care of the dead. I kept holding onto my mother's hand for a long time. I could not bring myself to let go of her hand. My sister and her daughters were attending to the requests my mother made before dying while the body was still warm. The white blouse had to be put on fast before the joints got stiff. I heard my sister giving instructions to her daughters, both of whom acted remarkably well in following her directions.

When her body was carried out, she wanted to go quietly into the night without disturbing her neighbors. Two nights before she died, she awakened from her sleep and asked my sister to call our brother so that he could start making the funeral arrangements including having her body picked up at night. That's when I learned about the white sheets she had been saving. She wanted to be wrapped in a white sheet after we dressed her. My mother in the hour of her death thought of other people's feelings, about neighbor's discomforts.

My mother died on September 8, 2005 at 6:20 p.m. We stayed with her through the night. At 2:30 a.m. with a candle lit by her side, we wrapped her in the white sheets and carried her out into the street.

Her burial took place in the same cemetery plot that held her husband who had died a few years earlier. Because the cemetery was filled beyond capacity, vertical burials had become the norm, with one body being placed above the body of another family member. My mother joked once: 'it will be my turn to be on top.'

Life goes on for the living. When I returned to America, seeing my son Daniel waiting for me with a bouquet of my favorite sunflowers made my heart give thanks.

Steve's Story

Steve is both a friend of mine as well as someone who does some handiwork for me. This marks the second year of his mother's descent into the death of her mind while her body lives on is how he describes her being afflicted with Alzheimer's disease

"If you knew my mother when she was alive, this is not how she wanted to go. I know if she knew what was in store for her, she would have taken a shotgun to herself. I don't even want to go visit her. She doesn't know who the fuck I am. She doesn't know shit. I might as well not exist as far as she is concerned. As for me, give me a massive one. The heart stops and I'm done. No waiting around for the end like a vegetable. But that's life. But what are you going to do? That's the deal of the deck".

I give Steve all my attention. By the look on his face, I can tell he knows I am listening to him. Other than telling him I'm sorry, or it must be difficult for you having to deal with your mother, there is not much to do but listen, which is no small deal. There are times when the best support we can give to someone else is to hold our tongue and just listen.

My private thoughts are in another realm. What I am thinking is that Alzheimer is seen as a disease because it is viewed as such by those outside of the experience of being a persona other than the one both self and others have known for so many years. Yet, the truth of the matter is that at any given point in time during our existence, the person we are known by is but one persona among the many selves within us we have chosen, albeit at times unaware of having done so, to give voice to.

Everything changes. Even who we are changes. Why? As time goes by and life's circumstances are not what they were previously, we change, mutate if you will, who we are, either consciously or unconsciously, in order to meet the differing circumstances of our lives as we pass from one stage of our lives to another. Seed, fetus, baby, infant, child, teenager, young adult, adult, middle age, old age and death are examples of the need to adapt who we are to be the person we need and are called upon to be, not he or she of the past, but in the present moment.

Might this not able be true of Alzheimer's disease? Perhaps, it is not so much a malady but a metamorphic process undergone in order to meet the needs of a person who will eventually die by virtue of becoming another persona to better cope with the fears, anxiety and challenges posed by the separation of death. In essence, I have a need to forget who I am and become accustomed to living in a different world now before I die if I am to let go of and be let go of who I no longer am at the time of my death with some sense of acceptance, resolution and peace.

Perhaps, we should not view Alzheimer's patients as forlorn, even crazed, but rather as different, traveling in an altered state of consciousness. If only there were nursing homes transformed into retreats, based on Aldous Huxley's beliefs about the kind of setting needed by the aged and the dying in order to remain sane, where, with the assistance of psychedelic drugs, residents could experience life's endings in the eyes of others not as zoo creatures, but rather as strangers in a strange land assisted by knowledgeable and skillful guides as they embark upon one of the most monumental journeys of their lives. To go from being alive to not being alive.

Char's Story

Saturday night. Paula and I are out on a date, sitting in a church listening to a sacred music concert performed by a friend of ours and her band. Intermission time. Char, who is in her sixties, a former co-worker of my wife before Paula retired from her position as a high school social worker, approaches us to exchange greetings. She asks how our summer went? Paula tells her we had a wonderful summer on Maui, and proceeds to ask Char if her summer had gone well?

She answers, "As best as I could make it. Being without my husband who was the love of my life since I was eighteen is not easy. I still cry. Even this evening hearing music played for those who have departed brought tears to my eyes. What am I to do? I'm making the best of it. As I said, he was the love of my life."

Is this not what either Paula or I as well as the surviving member of all other wedded couples whose love for one another has lasted the test of time will someday say when asked, how did your summer go? My answer would probably be quite similar to that of Char's. "I'm making the best of it." However, underneath those words in my internal dialogue, I am asking myself, "Am I going to make it?" Just the thought of being without Paula envelops my entire being with an almost unbearable sorrow and brings tears to my eyes.

I have often said that I wish to be the first to die. I cannot imagine my Paula going from she is to she was. I would not want to go on living with a heart crushed well beyond being broken. The possibility of a better tomorrow if I can just make it through today would not be sufficient enough reason for me to want to see yet another sunrise without Paula at my side.

Yes, it is courageous to go off to war knowing that many who do face the possibility of suffering wounds and loss. Is it not equally courageous to go off to love knowing that eventual wounding and loss is not a possibility, but a reality all lovers will face one day.

Barry's Story

By the time he was nineteen, Barry had become an accomplished killer, having taken the lives of at least five Vietnamese during the course of seeing action in Vietnam. The coup de grace for one being Barry shaking the man's brains out of his head, the top of which had been blown out by gunfire, onto the ground. While the men who had sent Barry off to a foreign land to maim and kill or be maimed or killed were drinking their double martinis in posh surroundings back home in the USA, Barry was eating his guts out as he trudged through what was once verdant and fertile land, but which now was dead and in a state of decay due to the lingering effects of Agent Orange and also reeked of burned and rotting flesh.

By the end of his tour in Vietnam, youthful Barry no longer existed. His Christian faith strewn on a waste dump by a Catholic chaplain whose pro-life position did not prevent him from telling Barry that when you are in uniform, the commandment reads as follows—thou shall kill, and not to feel any guilt or second thoughts about doing so for your country.

This young man's belief that his country valued human life above all else had been shattered by the experience of paying a rubber tree plantation owner a much larger sum of money for a rubber tree being irreparably damaged by a wayward artillery shell than he was authorized to pay a family for a husband and father lost as a result of collateral damage.

His body, mind and spirit weighed down by the burden of what he had witnessed and committed during his time in hell, Barry seemingly walked and talked as if he were alive, but he had become a shell of a man, filled with anger and despair of such a nature as to render him essentially lifeless within. To escape his demons, any drug would do. If sniffing horseshit would have done the trick, so be it.

Nobody spat on Barry upon his return to the states. Nobody cursed him out for being a baby killer. Nobody shunned him for doing the work of the devil. In fact, the long-haired, tie-dyed, Jimmy Hendrix music loving, marijuana smoking, make love not war hippies of northern California extended their arms and hearts to this very hurt soul brother whose country had turned him into an exile from his own humanity. They and the therapist he was seeing, both serving to temper the acid like memories eating away at his insides, allowed him to process his pain and anger to the degree that he was able to tolerate living.

Some forty odd years later, Barry still suffers from his Vietnam experience, but not to such a degree that he yearns to join the one hundred thousand plus veterans of the war who have committed suicide since their return home. The things they carried back from the war residing in their minds and hearts being too great a burden to bear, making death a preferred choice over living.

Active in the peace and justice movement, Barry is a regular guest speaker in the Peace Studies class I teach, educating young men and women about the realities of war and urging them to stand and be counted in the pursuit of peace and justice. Speaking with disciplined passion, he shares what it is like to walk through the valley of the shadow of death and to be stuck there in the darkness, not able to see the light serving as a guidepost to the end of this harrowing journey. Some give up. Others come to the realization that they must engage in the necessary work to find or construct the light within themselves. No piece of cake, to be certain. However, to paraphrase an ancient proverb: "Give a man a fish and he will be dependent on you. Teach a man how to fish and he will never go hungry."

Almost always Barry closes his presentation by telling my students that no matter what they are or will be facing in their lives, to keep their eyes on the prize, which is the human potential to confront evil being inflicted on others in our name and to be willing to walk the talk of peace and justice. He shares with them his belief that to look fear in the face and do what needs to be done is not so much an act of courage as it is an act of necessity if, at the end of your life, you want to be able to say, I have no regrets, for I followed the teachings of my heart and mind.

Here is a man who speaks of a time of dying that he was once enmeshed in and swallowed up by, leaving his audience more knowledgeable as well as stunned by death and destruction tales known as war. A man who encountered the enemy outside of himself and the enemy within, our shadow side that both darkens and lessens our lives. A man who knows purgatory exists on earth as well as in the beyond. A man who knows all too intimately and well that one can feel dead while still alive. Here also is a man who, albeit hurting, is courageous enough to choose to let his life unfold, notwithstanding its trials and tribulations, in lieu of surrendering to death's siren call with its promise of "no more."

Alejandro's and Louis's Story

We had never seen each other before. Yet, after just a few minutes spent talking with one another, I knew I had met a kindred soul, a man who spoke freely of the bravery of the heart. Upon hearing that I taught a course on death and dying and had written of my mother's having to bury two of her sons, he shook his head from side to side, indicating how wrong that was, and said, "Never should a parent have to endure such suffering. For a parent to endure the death of a child violates the order of the universe."

"Yes," I responded, "rather I give my lungs, my kidneys, even my heart to my child that he or she might live is what I would willingly do should that be necessary to spare their lives."

Alejandro replied, "I would give my arms, my eyes, my skin, anything of mine, if that be necessary to my child." He went on to say, "I have endured suffering in my life, but to put your child in a grave is beyond suffering. To experience that would be agony beyond relief."

Our exchange of words was followed by silence. I could hear his deep breathing as I am sure he could hear mine. Was it because we had gone to a place in the realm of imagination where life's possibilities makes one feel as if he were drowning, gasps of breath marking the end of a life?

It was clear to me that Alejandro and I knew one of life's essential truths. It is our presence not our presents that our children want and need above all the gifts that fathers can bestow upon their offspring. And if that is to mean in the form of our very own flesh and blood, so be it. Should fathers not be willing to do for their children what all mother's do?

Paula E's Story

During the day Paula E is a librarian, catering to the research needs of students at Columbia College Chicago as well as being a mother hen to those young men and women who are in need of nurturing. Come many nights and weekends, she assumes her other identity, that of being a saint. For she is a hospice volunteer offering unto the dying a final gift—to afford those who are withering on the vine and about to be separated from the tree of life, a sense of dignity and recognition that they matter, that they are of worth notwithstanding exterior appearance and loss of life's titles at work and at home. And she does this lovingly and selflessly within the context of do unto others as you would wish others to do unto you.

Fingers bejeweled with rings of vibrant colors to remind those who are about to receive her services of the beauty they can choose to cast their eyes upon even as they breathe their last breath. Whether it be to divert attention from fear and suffering, or to depart in the presence of. beauty, she graces those who are dying with one of life's greatest gifts—to be touched and held in the arms of love.

Each semester Paula E is a guest presenter in my Death and Dying Class, sharing with my students why someone would choose to be of service to the dying, and what is received as well as given in the process. She tells them of the many tears she has shed in the presence of the sorrow that life's endings can evoke among the dying and their loved ones; and of the smile on her face when inadvertently coming upon the very conservative and straight man who now takes great glee when lifting his gown to expose himself to whomever appears in his room, or the couple making love, a paean to life, on what is supposed to be a death bed.

Paula E is a living embodiment of the compassionate Buddha who knows that soul work also includes gentle human touch, a warm embrace, a good laugh, and, when necessary, the magic cure of hearty chicken soup spiced with sugar, metaphorically speaking, in its various forms.

As the generation of leaves,
So is that of men.

Homer

Voices From The Grave Story

There are times that the dead reach out to us, a collective us numbering in the hundreds of millions. If only we were to listen to their message, life on earth would be more merciful and compassionate. I was reminded of this truth upon viewing a documentary film on the life of Picasso on PBS, in which a story unfolded centered not on a war of the past, but rather on a war of present times.

In 1937 during the Spanish Civil War, Guernica, the most ancient town of Basques and the center of their cultural tradition, was reduced to rubble by a powerful fleet of German Lutwaffe and Italian Fascist League airplanes. The bombardment lasted for hours unleashing a rain of death and destruction consisting of bombs and other incendiary projectiles. Fighter planes plunged low from above the center of the town to machine-gun those of the civilian population who had taken refuge in the field. At the end of day, the whole of Guernica lay in flames with mangled bodies strewn all over.

Picasso's rendition of what occurred that day vividly captured and epitomized the horror of war and the suffering war inflicts upon individuals. This monumental work of art has transcended the bounds of a single time and place, becoming a timeless reminder of man's inhumanity unleashed upon his fellow humans as well as an anti-war symbol and a call for peace.

It is the year 2003. Colin Powell, U.S. Secretary of State, about to hold a press conference at United National headquarters in New York City explaining the Bush Administration's call for a war against Iraq, is standing at the podium. To his astonishment, he notices in the background a large replica of Picasso's Guernica. Alarmed by the thought that his words of war against the enemy would be filtered through the images of dead bodies of innocent men, women and children, voices crying out in horror and arms reaching out for deliverance from death's messengers, his staff orders that Guernica be completely covered over by a curtain lest the American public be disturbed by what war means in reality.

Yes, graves can hide bodies but not their memories, which serve as an eternal reminder of an essential truth if life on earth is to be more heaven than hell. Humans are not collateral damage. It is before, not after, all is said and done that we need to guide our actions in accordance with our knowing that we are all brothers and sisters. We are one family. The human family.

If only we would listen.

Paul Newman's Story

Handsome, virile, hot and forever young Paul Newman is gone. How can this be? He was Cool Hand Luke just a moment ago, and now he is stone cold dead. Is this not proof enough that death knows no boundaries, calling all, including the seeming invincible, to their inevitable rendezvous with life's endings.

What good can result from acknowledging such a reality? Well, if dying is what fate has in store even for those we look up to as gods, we, mere mortals that we are, have to know in our guts, hearts and the deepest recesses of our minds that our tickets are also going to be punched one day by Mr. Death. And the days of our lives pass by so quickly as we age. So, while there is a need for time to rest in order to gain the fortitude to go on with a life, the time of our lives is too brief and precious to let our lives go to waste.

A wasted life is a kind of death. Unlived potential and unlived dreams deteriorate and decay, just like a dead body, within us. After a while, the stench of death in the form of resentment, jealousy, envy, anger, withdrawal, wishing ill unto others and self permeates the space that an unlived life occupies.

Paul was quite aware of the relationship between a wasted life and death having experienced the tragic loss of his son who seemingly was never really able to fully get into this challenging thing called life. Perhaps, that is why Paul took up racecar driving with an unbridled passion. To remind all of us that you keep on truckin' no matter what. Nobody ever promised us a rose garden on our life journey. Besides, the sweetest smelling roses have the sharpest thorns.

Love's Story

Love is the great slayer.

To lose someone we love and who loves us is perhaps life's greatest tragedy. To not love a loved one to the ultimate degree possible, or not allow a loved one to love us to the fullest extent possible, is also a major life tragedy, denying love's transformative power the opportunity to revitalize our lives. Why is this so? Because love, having two sides, the universal yin and yang, is both the great giver of life worth living and the great slayer of life in need of dying.

Let love into our lives and that which has lain dormant within us, seeds filled with life's possibilities will sprout with a passion as our life unfolds. Let love into our lives and we will know of the heaven to be found on earth and what it feels like to be dancing among the stars. Let love into our lives and its fire will, day in and out, burn away at the hurts, pains disappointments, insecurities and fears housed within us until they, irrespective of source or nature, yield to the greater force. Let love into our lives and its unbridled fierceness will serve to keep at bay whomever and whatever should dare attempt to stop its energizing forces flow within us.

There are times when our physical selves needs to be cut into in order to get to that part of our beings in need of repair and healing by the hands of a skilled surgeon wielding a scalpel. It is also true that the defenses we erect against feeling in the hope that these protective layers would keep our hearts from once again being hurt must also be cut into to expose that part of our emotional selves in need of repair and healing. However, this time it is by the intensely pulsating light and energy of love.

Yes, as we know, love has its feminine aspect, its soft side, but love also has its masculine aspect, its fierce side. I know this well, having been burnt by Paula's love, its hot molten fire seeping inside of me to all my secret hiding places where my fears reside. At such moments, it as if she is no longer external, as if all of her is within me. At such moments, I am being held and comforted and healed.

Love is the great teacher. Its presence speaking the great truth that life is beautiful and magic is everywhere.

This world will be destroyed
also the mighty ocean
will dry up;
and this broad earth
will be burnt up.
Therefore . . .
cultivate compassion.

Buddhaghosa, *Visusddhi-magga*

Earth's Story

If I were to see a flower growing near a sidewalk, it's more than just what I observe. All that exists, everything in this world is contributing to the flower's growth. The soil that the flower planted in, the air around it, the rain from the sky, the light from the sun, all are working together to bring this flower to life.

If I were to draw a circle in the grass, place myself in the center of the circle, and observe only that which occurs inside of the circle after a moment or two, I would become aware that there are several different insects crawling on me. A spider on my sleeve, an ant of my hand, a ladybug on my scarf, and soon other small unidentifiable green creatures will have landed on my shoulder. As I observe their behavior, I start to think of my relationship to these organisms at that moment in the context of my being their landscape. I note that I was somewhat fearful when the spider began to crawl up my sleeve, tightening my shirt around my wrist in an attempt to prevent it from reaching my skin. I started to think of what it would be like if I were to be covered by insects crawling all over me, demanding access into areas where I wouldn't willingly allow admittance, biting me, releasing venoms into my skin and blood stream. Breaking into a sweat, breathing accelerated and irregular, heart racing, body poisoned by stress hormones and adrenaline. My immune system, weakened by such a state of distress, I would become less capable of fending off such an unrelenting attack. I realize that just as a human being's natural mechanisms of maintaining health and well being can be eventually exhausted, so can the earth's.

Dying and death are universal forces at play not only in the realm of the human experience, but in all of existence, including the earth itself. Apocalyptic visions of the world coming to an end have been one of the most common themes to be found in the annals of science fiction writing. Whether consumed by fire and brimstone in the form of a blast and fallout from nuclear weapons, or from storms and flooding of a ferocious and catastrophic nature, the likes of which we have never experienced on earth before or since the time of Noah, earth as we have known it, a life support system for human existence, is doomed to suffer a violent demise.

The other primary theme to be found in science fiction writing is that of a future best described as a human version of an ant colony or beehive. In this scenario, we read about masses of humans, better seen as automatons, busy as ants or bees going about their lives in accordance with their assigned functions without either mind or heart being brought into play as tools of reflection. Here we have despotic regimes keeping their citizens in line and on task using fear and punishment as well as other forms of repression to curb dissent.

In either case, what is described is a future in which the human species will experience transition from a pulsating life force in the form of living and breathing participatory democracies, albeit imperfect, to totalitarian regimes. In essence, the ending, or death, of a way of life that elevates the human journey, and the emergence of a "new human" living out a version of George Orwell's *Animal Farm,* where war is peace and darkness is light.

Also common to these depictions of the future is the presence of aliens watching and hovering above us, waiting for the right time to invade and conquer planet earth. However, just as death is an integral part of our journey, an unfolding of the human program stored within us, and not an external force coming to get us, might it be so that the alien is not that which is external. To the contrary, in such a context, might alien not mean that which is strange to us in the sense of a positive force challenging us to believe and act in a transformative manner; that is, to have at the hub of the wheel on which the world turns compassion, nurturing and sharing as contrasted to exploitation and greed.

What is the nature of this alien? It is the creative and connecting life force within us, waiting to be birthed from our bodies. However, before the birthing there is the pregnancy period, in which the "pregnant" human carries the "child," learning in the process that compassion, nurturing and sharing are life's bedrock.

In order for swords to be willingly given up for plowshares, for the embracing of others to be assigned greater value and awarded a greater proportion of the world's wealth than the killing of others, the time is well past due for life on earth as practiced by humans ever since the masculine subjugated the feminine to come to an end. The known, a hyper-testosterone charged male centered world culture must surrender to a higher order of being, in which the breast has replaced the fist as a symbol of the human journey on earth; in which Mary (in her various forms across cultures) giving birth, the generative principle, and not Christ on the Cross (in his various forms across cultures), the degenerative principle, serves as the hub of the wheel on which civilizations travel.

Who would benefit from an earth honored, respected and lived in harmony with? Of course, the living. Of course, the dying. To die in an institutionalized setting amidst needles and tubes surrounded by concrete and drywall cut off from all natural surroundings is not exactly what the dying need. Letting go of our bodies can be fearful and anxiety provoking enough.

At the time of departure, those who are dying need to be in the presence of unlimited, not limited, freedom.

The earth offers us so much beauty. Unending stands of trees, poplar, pine, elm, sycamore, maple, willow, and black walnut. Black, brown and white mushrooms and toadstools. Blue, orange, red, mauve, purple and yellow wildflowers. Raspberries, blackberries, huckleberries, dewberries and blueberries. Buckwheat and oats. Flat land, rolling land, dry land and wetland. Huge white clouds floating in a big blue sky.

I sit myself at the foot of an aged tree, mother and crone being its essence. Bark is missing in places. A few limbs are twisted giving off the appearance of gnarled hands while others have succumbed to disease, lightning or just age. Woodpeckers carve out notches in the trunk in their search for insect food. Ants scurry back and forth on the lower limbs. Birds bring food to their young waiting in nests in the upper limbs. Apple bud blossoms are opening. Save for a slightly warm wind blowing in from the south causing the leaves of the tree and the field of oats and buckwheat to dance slowly, the melodic and soulful singing of birds, and the fluttering wings of a stoned on nectar butterfly, there is silence.

Trees do not cry out for notice and attention. Trees do not have pretense and wear costumes to hide what they are. Trees do not perform community service to save the planet by engaging in good works after 5 p.m. and on weekends to undo the damage that 9-5 work has inflicted on the planet. Trees are just there all the time doing their thing, planet support work—holding the earth together, housing and feeding life, transmuting noxious and poisonous vapors into life giving air, offering shade from the hot sun, beautifying the lands with their presence, reminding us that sometimes just being there, just being part of the community of life, is all that is needed.

I sit beneath the tree. I do not give my mind over to how this tree can be of use to me? I wonder how I can serve and learn from this elder, how I can dwell in its majesty? Closing my eyes, I begin to rock back and forth on the balls and heels of my feet as waves of energy released from the tree float towards where I sit, bathing me with wisdom and peacefulness, impregnating me with nature's grace. Peace above me. Peace below me. Peace all around me.

To die amidst the presence of the living planet Earth, on a day with sun shining under a clear blue sky as one reposes in a meadow filled with wildflowers of heavenly scents swaying gently in the wind, or under moonlight beneath a mysterious starlit sky promising a return home rather than a trek into the unknown, is a blessing, a gift from the gods and goddesses. Let us, at the end of our lives, be filled with a sense of existence beyond time so that our brief, flickering lives may take comfort in knowing that the flame of our essence never ceases to be lit. No end to the sky. No end to the ocean.

It is within the poetry of nature that our spirits are lifted beyond the challenges of the day, of our lives, when we are living and when we are dying.

Dying, Death and Consciousness

If I conceive of death as something coming at me, to get me, then I am terrified. But death does not come to take me. I am it.

Stanley Keleman, *Living Your Dying*

L ET US GAZE into the realm of an alternative to the normative mass consciousness culture of dying, away from a technologized, institutionalized, and dehumanized way of facing dying and death. For such a modernized version of what constitutes dying and death results neither in an acceptance of the inevitable nor in an openness, as in the case of birth, to one of life's great journeys. To the contrary, and to the detriment of those who are facing life's endings, it instills fear and dread within those who are dying and their loved ones.

In direct opposition to the prevalent image of death and dying portrayed in the mass media, the primary educational instrument of modern times, that death comes from the outside, as something that happens to us, the truth is we know how to die. Our bodies know how to die. Dying, like birthing, is something we know how to do. We have been doing it as long as humans have existed on earth, an integral part of the natural process of a life. Letting go of our lives without fear is to surrender to our bodies guiding force as we merge with the eternal source.

Keleman takes the concept of the body as a knowledgeable and wise teacher in our lives one major step further. Stressing the principle that life incarnate is a continual process of individual human experience manifesting in the body, he states, "We do not have bodies, we are our bodies." According to Keleman, the matrix known as the biosphere is comprised of all life forms. Upon examining the embryological process, we see this marvelous sphere of fertilized ovum beginning to multiply as the whole biosphere develops into a body.

He goes to say that the biosphere is made up of all bodies, including our own, a part of a gigantic living matrix, and that collective humanity is like the cells of the planetary body. I am called Louis, but at my core I am a living process organizing itself into that which is known as Louis. While death ends a specific configuration around my life, it doesn't end a life process. Mind, filled with institutionalized religious, societal and cultural instilled fears and hallucinations, wishes to remain in control, to remain dominant, needs to step aside, and allow body to guide us through the natural occurrence of dying, a path that we know how to travel on.

In the allegory that is popularly known as Plato's cave story, a group of figures are sitting in a cave with their eyes fixed on images on the wall and with their backs towards the entrance. Viewing their shadows cast upon the wall by the flickering flames of a fire burning behind them, and mistaking these shadows for reality, they remain imprisoned, a captive of their thoughts, never turning to see the light shining through the opening to the cave, never venturing beyond their misperceptions of reality into experiencing reality itself.

One of the great fears of dying has to do with separation anxiety, to be cut off from others, to be no longer connected with life. This is an understandable fear, but is a product of a cultural dominant teaching that at my core, I am alone in the universe. Yet, sages and spiritual teachers of diverse origins have offered unto humanity a quite different conception of what in is to be a human being. Namely, what is perceived as the individuated self is not separate in any sense or form from the rest of creation, but is in fact coextensive with all that exists, an interconnected web of all living things. In contrast to keeping those who are dying locked in the prison of enduring death as an intruder into our lives rather than surrendering to the inevitable, death is not seen as the end of existence, but, rather, as a transition or crossing over, whereby the dying individual is experiencing altered states of consciousness. Often this is realized before ones death by means of psychedelics (mind-manifesting substances) or other consciousness transformative means.

Experiencing such altered states of awareness during which one "lives through" the process of dying and the death journey impresses upon the individual, who now possesses experiential knowledge of what it means to leave the world of bodily existence, the realization that we, at our core, are not just our bodies. Such experiences provide insight into the possible transcendental nature of the dying and death experience, turning it into a living experience of an extraordinary nature.

For those whose minds are open to considering the possibility that, just as how we take in and make sense of the world of the living is dependent on the perceptual lens we choose to wear when interacting with the world of the living, how we take in and make sense of the world of the dying is equally dependent on the perceptual lens we put on during those times. Michael Warner, in *Ways of the Shaman*, speaks to the role of cognicentrism likely to be present in our interactions with the world. Cognicentrism, as he defines it, being equivalent to ethnocentrism when viewing cultures other than our own. However, it is not the limitations of being enmeshed in our own culture that is the deciding factor at play here, but the limitations of our experiences in the realms of consciousness.

Stanislav Grof, who has extensive experience working with dying populations using psychedelics to ease the transition between life and death, writing in *The Ultimate Journey: Consciousness and the Mystery of Death*, enlightens us to the reality that:

> . . . *research with holotropic states has added a second major experiential domain to mainstream psychiatry's cartography of the human psyche: the transpersonal, meaning literally 'beyond the personal' or 'transcending the personal.' Experiences on this level involve transcending the usual boundaries of the body/ ego and the limitations of three-dimensional space and linear time, which restrict our perception of the world in the ordinary state of consciousness.*
>
> *Transpersonal experiences can be divided into three categories. The first involves primarily transcending*

the usual spatial barriers, of the limitations of the skin-encapsulated ego. Typical examples are merging with another person into a state that can be called 'dual unity,' assuming the identity of another person, or identifying with the consciousness of an entire group of people (e.g., all mothers of the world . . .). A person may even experience an extension of consciousness so enormous that it seems to encompass all of humanity, the entire human species.

In the second case, we are able to witness or experientially identify with something that is not ordinarily accessible to our senses, something that is considered not humanly possible to experience.

The third category of transpersonal experiences is even stranger. Here consciousness seems to extend into realms and dimensions that the Western industrial culture does not consider 'real.' . . . In its farthest reaches, individual consciousness can identify with cosmic consciousness of the Universal Mind known under many different names—Brahman, Buddha, the Cosmic Christ, Allah, the Tao, The Great Spirit, Anima Mundi, and many others. The ultimate of all experiences appears to be identification with the Supracosmic and Metacosmic Void, the mysterious and primordial emptiness and nothingness that is conscious of itself and is the ultimate cradle of all existence.

During a peak experience, we have a sense of overcoming the usual fragmentation of the mind and body and feel that we reached a state of unity and wholeness. We experience . . . an ecstatic union with

humanity, nature, the cosmos, and God. In the process
we feel intense joy, bliss, serenity and inner peace.

For an experiential account of allowing the natural process
of dying to have its way, let us turn once again to Grinspoon
and Bakalar where we read in *Psychedelic Drugs Reconsidered*
of the dying experience of Aldous Huxley:

> *But on the morning of November twenty-second,*
> *a Friday, it became clear the gap between living and*
> *dying was closing . . . At ten in the morning, an almost*
> *inaudible Aldous asked for paper and scribbled 'If I*
> *go,' and then some directions about his will. It was his*
> *first admission that he might die . . . 'At this point there*
> *is so little to share,' he told her, a statement that she*
> *interpreted as meaning no questions. Around noon he*
> *asked for the pad of paper and scribbled.*

> *'LSD—try it*
> *intramuscular*
> *100mm'*

> *In a letter circulated among Aldous's friends, Laura*
> *Huxley described what followed: You know very well the*
> *uneasiness in the medical mind about this drug. But no*
> *authority, not even an army of authorities, could have*
> *stopped me then. I went into Aldous's room with the*
> *vial of LSD and prepared a syringe. The doctor asked*
> *me if I wanted him to give the shot—maybe because*
> *he saw that my hands were trembling. His asking me*

made me conscious of my hands, and I said, 'No, I must do this.'

An hour later she gave Huxley a second 100mm. Then she began to talk, bending close to his ear, whispering, 'light and free you let go darling; forward and up. You are going forward and up; you are going toward the light. Willingly and consciously you are going, willing and consciously, and you are doing this beautifully; you are going toward the light—you are going toward a greater love . . . You are going toward Maria's love with my love. You are going toward a greater love than you have ever known. You are going toward the best, the greatest love, and it is easy, it is so easy, and you are doing it so beautifully.'

All struggle ceased. The breathing became slower and slower and slower, until, like a piece of music just finishing so gently in sempre piu piano, dolcamente, at twenty post five in the afternoon, Aldous Huxley died.

During psychedelic induced journeys into the realms of dying and death, my experiences have served to affirm what my bother Edward, who had traveled into transcendental realms of consciousness for many years, shared with me prior to his death. "Louis, I have no fear of dying because I know by virtue of my experiential journeys into consciousness that I am more than my body, that the essence of 'I' will continue to exist once my corporeal body ceases to house my consciousness"

What follows are selections from journal writings based on my experiences while under the influence of psychedelics relevant to life's endings.

Lounging on my bed, I envision primordial forests teeming with ghostlike dwellings inhabited by figures resembling humans wearing threadbare robes with hoods covering decayed faces. Descending from the gray charcoal sky are mammoth birds of prey with huge purplish black bodies and rhinestone beaks, each bird a work of terror as can be seen in the eyes of the creatures with decayed faces, eyes that are quickly gouged out by bird claws and eaten.

I realize I am walking through the valley of death, the dead remains of myself left over from past experiences that have left me feeling hurt and disappointed with life. I say to myself, 'Oh, woe is me, what am I to do?' Breathe, breathe it all away, is the answer received in response to my question. Chanting 'asat chit ananda', I slowly breathe in, hold, breathe out, hold, repeating this sequence over and over until breathing and awareness merge into a unity. One by one, the human like figures and the birds disappear. I am left alone amidst the ghostlike dwellings, now filled with starlight and a joyous occupant. It is I.

*   *   *

Although she is not physically present, she is sitting beside me. 'Just breathe,' I say to her, 'let yourself become aware of that which is here, always here, beyond the veil of the reality of the moment.'

A figure, bird-like, most primitive in nature and appearance, violet blue in color, hovers above me. I sense it poses no threat and accept its presence. The ground beneath my feet is swirling around as the surrounding cliffs and valleys, timeless in nature, beckon to me to be with them, to acknowledge and accept their gift of eternity, to enlarge my sense of reality.

Death's specter is near. I accept its presence. It asks, 'Am I willing to give up the life I am living that our home might be filled with life?' However, at this stage of my existence, death does not desire my physical life; rather, it longs for my negativity. That is the price I must pay as my contribution to our house being a home. Happiness wishes to be present in our family. We are all tired of and worn down by the fussing and fighting.

I vow to give up my attachment to negativity out of my love for my family.

My thoughts turn to my darling wife. I know I am to just accept her for who she is, to just love her as she is, to let her be the beautiful flowering blossom and gift of pure joy that she is. I tell her I am sorry for hurting her and ask for her forgiveness.

She speaks to me of her vulnerability, how she opened herself up to me, and how I have both loved and hurt her deeply. We embrace each other. We begin to cry, salty tears of regret and joy. Gazing into the eternity of her eyes, I flow into blue space where color and I merge into one.

*   *   *

Ambling over to Dad as tree, I sit myself down at the base of his trunk. At his memorial service, his ashes were intermingled with the roots of a Jackfruit tree that began to bear breadfruit once it achieved maturity. With Dad, I need to do a lot of forgiving and healing because he along with our mother were at the root of our family, and his healing would contribute to the healings of his sons, living and dead. I tell him of the hurt and pain he inflicted upon his sons as he acted out the craziness of his own pain carried forward into his adult life from childhood sufferings, of my forgiveness of him, and ask of him that he forgive me for the hurt and pain I gave to him in return. We both cry, he with shedding leaves, I with salty tears.

Just as a clearing of the atmosphere can follow rain, I can seem more clearly now after my rain of tears has ceased flowing. The price of not forgiving and allowing oneself to be forgiven is to be walled up inside a high security prison, cut off from the trials and tribulations and heartbreak of life, but also from life's passions and joys. Safe, but also forlorn. Yes, I can see more clearly now, but the clarity is one of acceptance of life as shadow and light, of mud as well as sky, of life as is and not as should be.

I turn away and walk over to a eucalyptus tree. Resting my weary body against its trunk, I tear a few leaves, releasing their healing aroma that I breathe in deeply, and with each exhalation I blow its curative powers towards my tree family.

Is life not blessed!

*   *   *

Cities of multi-hued splendor, each structure bearing a golden minaret, arise out of the sea under a clear sky, while I, standing amidst verdant forests overflowing with white ginger, heliconia, hibiscus, orchids and love in full bloom, am enraptured and still, listening to the conversation of creation surrounding me. I need neither church, nor synagogue, nor mosque, nor altar, for this, the great outdoors, is my place of worship, my shrine. Lying down on the moss-covered earth, the sound of waves gently breaking on the shore serving as my sacred music, I fall asleep, for minutes, or months, or years.

Awakening, I am met by a completely changed sky, dark gray, soon to find myself being enveloped by a gray cloud, feeling as if I am being taken over by death, that I am dying. Panic and fear begin to take hold of me. My life is in the grasp of death. Remembering that all is one, that life and death are not separate, that all of human experience is contained within the seamless web of existence, that dying and death are known to me, that there is no beginning and no end, that I never was and always will be, I take heed of her advice, her words of wisdom—'My darling, always remember to breathe.'

Breathing consciously with deep inhalations and exhalations, chanting 'asat chit ananda,' I visualize life entering me in the form of an inhalation and death leaving me as an exhalation. Panic and fear subside, replaced by quietude, a soothing, a calmness.

The dark gray clouds dissipate, supplanted by an azure sky. I lift myself off of the ground. It is time for me to go home.

*   *   *

I walk on the land. It is time to dance with the sun. My body moves harmoniously within the realms of liberation, of freedom, of wonder, in sync with the life energy being released by the golden sphere, a vibrating and pulsating circle of light, giving off cleansing heat and passion fire to my mind. We all need to sunbathe mind as much as body, letting it air out in the purifying presence of natural heat.

Noticing a piece of sugar cane on the ground, and imagining it to be a sword, I engage in a fencing duel with my father, the jackfruit tree, piercing his heart. The hurt, the pus, the bile run out, and the tree becomes more vibrant, lighter, its branches now sporting a lilt that reaches out toward the sky. Dad must acquire the discipline to stay with the forces of light, and close himself off from the forces of darkness.

I immerse myself in a song and dance routine. I being Fred Astaire and myriad trees, fantail palms, coconut, banana, lemon, lime, avocado, eucalyptus, bamboo, coffee, Surinam cherry, passion fruit . . . being my partners. We have so much fun together.

Joe, my brother, now a hibiscus tree overflowing with vibrantly luscious pink blossoms with yellow stalks, beckons unto me. I ask his forgiveness for being judgmental, of not accepting who he was and the life he led as his choice. I also ask of him to bless me with the riches that he possessed and still possesses—a sunny disposition.

I return to the house to shower for my family shall be returning soon. Lighting pure white candles and pine incense, I begin preparing dinner—grilled salmon with steamed potatoes and mixed greens salad topped off with coconut slices and cranberries.

From the viewpoint of the kitchen window, I look out at an infinite blue sky, with a cotton puff of a cloud here and there. As I become enthralled in the moment, a cloud seemingly dissolves into the sky. It is no longer cloud but sky, filling me with the thought that one day it shall be my time—the form that embodies my essence to dissolve into life. Death, I realize, is not that which exists outside of me, a terror that comes and takes me away on a foreboding journey to oblivion. To the contrary, death is a part of me just as birth was. I know death as I know birth. I know how to die as I know how to be born.

As cloud returns to sky and as wave returns to ocean, I shall come to rest in a quite familiar place, and reside there in peace.

*   *   *

It is sunrise. I lie down on a large black and gray boulder with a calm sea by my side and a bright orange sun shining down from above. With eyes shut, I see grotesque, hideous, snarling and crazed put bulls running towards me. I am not afraid. Holding my ground, I smile and send love to those forces welling up from inside of me. Dark and ugly aspects of myself that

*have been my life-long companions, but which I need
no longer to possess.*

*The dogs turn into white doves, encircling me as they
weave leis of yellow flowers representing healing, blue
flowers representing clarity, purple flowers representing
passion, and white flowers representing purity. My wife,
daughter and son chant 'asat chit ananda' over and
over again so that no sound of the universe but theirs
is to be heard.*

*Slowly, in turn each of my loved ones, approaches,
sits down as close to me as possible, takes my hands in
theirs, touches their lips to mine, and with conscious and
deliberate intent breathes love into my open and receptive
mouth. The body armor that has been my way of keeping
out the world of intimacy from entering too deeply into
my space breaks apart and falls from my body. Walls
come tumbling down. A bridge appears above the moat
of separation from others that has been my companion
ever since my childhood, allowing those who love me
to cross over and enter my life with a deepness I have
never known before.*

*Emerging from my mother's womb is a child with
blissful light at his essence. Crawling away from her
body, so that a few feet separate us from one another,
I begin to throw up. Piece after piece of foul smelling
pus covered slime emerges from within me, striking
the ground with a hissing noise. I collect my vile
outpourings into a pile, take a match to it setting it
ablaze, transforming all that which is negative inside
of my mind, body and soul into smoke that I neither*

inhale or allow to cloud my eyes, thus preventing me from seeing life's joys and beauty.

Words come. I tell myself, 'Give up the struggle. Why continue to resist being who I truly am? It is no use to pretend otherwise. I can take whatever crap I want to heap on myself and still love myself. Why not walk in the light with strength of character, compassion and beauty as my constant companions?'

Thunder and lightning resound and break through the sky. A warm rain begins to fall. Pain, sorrow and life's lost loves are cleared from my being. The rain ceases. A glorious multicolored rainbow of orange, red, orange, blue green and purple arches from end of the valley to the other.

I am ready to go home. It is time for me to be with my loved ones. I am ready and open to embracing and being embraced by life.

My Death and Dying Class

IN THE SUMMER of 2001, following the passing of my mother, I began offering a class on the subject of death and dying to the students of Columbia College Chicago, where I have taught for almost forty years. When I first broached the idea of including such a class among the college's summer class offerings, I was advised by some of my colleagues to rename the course. In their minds, to keep the present title would prove to be a kiss of death in terms of enrolling sufficient students to make the class viable; that is, attract sufficient students to meet the minimum enrollment. In their words, "who would want to spend summer evenings dealing with such a morbid subject?"

Well, I obviously struck into a need and desire vein of great depth waiting to be mined because, within a couple of days of the opening of registration for summer classes, the class was closed due to the maximum number of students allowed having registered for it, an enrollment pattern that has remained the same each subsequent summer the course has been offered. As attested to by both formal and informal student evaluations and other forms of student feedback, it has earned the reputation of being, "a must take before you graduate course because it will change your life" in the student grapevine. Why? Due to it being a life transforming and life enhancing experience for those who are open and courageous enough to explore the subject of death and dying with Louis, which is how I am known by my students, as their guide and mentor.

The class is based on the premise that the study of death and dying affords us the opportunity to go on a reflective/experiential journey to the center of our beings in the process of facing some of life's eternal questions: Where did I come from? Who am I? Why am I here? Where am I going? How do I wish to get there? As such constituted, the class is an inquiry into the nature of human existence through the prism of studying living and dying, life and death. It has been said by the wise that we will die as we have lived; that how we experience living is how we will experience dying; that what is found now is found then.

By opening themselves up to go beyond their fears as they engage in a study of their final journey as embodied beings, and allowing minds to acknowledge and hearts to feel the reality that they and everyone they love and are loved by in return will become dust in the wind, my students experience an awakening to life's preciousness. For the heart of the matter is that just to live, to touch and feel, to laugh and cry, to be sad and happy, to love and be loved, are holy blessings.

Yet all such treasures, dependent on human interaction, are often taken for granted, or even depreciated amidst modern culture's focus on as well as idolization of the material world. Acceptance of the inevitability of mortality for all and the uncertainty of when death will occur staring in their faces compels my students to give thoughtful reconsideration to what they truly value above all else in their lives and what would cause them to suffer the greatest loss? The gold in their lives is usually called mom, dad, brother, sister, grandma, grandpa, friend, boyfriend, girlfriend . . .

My approach to teaching is best described as student centered inquiry within a framework of a set of objectives that I believe are at the core of a course of study on the subject of death and dying. Students are encouraged to formulate and ask questions that are meaningful to them, and do not necessarily have easy answers. Lastly, students are both encouraged and required to take what they learned beyond the classroom as they engage loved ones in exploring life's endings.

Course objectives are as follows:

- ◆ To study the effects of mass media (print, audio and visual) portrayals of death and dying on our understanding of and practices related to life's endings.
- ◆ To study the teachings of major philosophical, societal, cultural, psychological, religious/spiritual and transformative consciousness traditions in relation to knowledge, ideas, values and practices associated with death and dying.
- ◆ To address fundamental challenges to be found at the center of our lives; e.g., transience, doubt, vulnerability, loss, challenge and the meaning and purpose of the human journey on earth, raised by confronting our mortality and other forms of life's endings.

◆ To reflect upon how we experience, take in, give order to, make sense of, find meaning in and learn to live life more fully by virtue of our encounters with life's endings in our lives and in the lives of our loved ones?

◆ To initiate a dialogue with our loved ones on their relationship to death and dying in order to establish/reinforce a channel of communication on a subject requiring a mode of interchange supportive of honesty and compassion; and to learn how to utilize this mode of interchange when dealing with other forms of life's endings.

◆ To formulate in the form of a class project to be presented to the class a vision of death and dying reflective of what one has learned during the course of study.

In fulfillment of the in-class presentations, students have recited poetry and other forms of writings of their own making, shown their drawings, photographs and videos, played music they have composed, and danced works they have choreographed among other creative forms of expression. Two presentations stand out in my mind for reasons of creativity, quality of work and impact on classmates.

Annie, a woodworker, built a coffin starting from scratch using discarded lumber. When asked why the discarded lumber, she responded, "Even those deemed not worthy of recognition originated as stardust, and they too shine on once their lives are over."

The coffin was lined with a faux silk material, taken from a dress especially favored by her mother who had died the previous year from breast cancer. It also contained a built-in small mirror to be best seen if one were lying in the coffin. Inviting her classmates to place themselves inside the coffin and imaging themselves to be dead, those who took Annie up on offer were instructed by Annie to view themselves in the mirror.

When asked why she placed the mirror in the coffin, Annie replied, "So we can realize that each of us are mortal and need to construct our lives to be as well made as our coffins."

The second presentation was the work of Shelby, a fashion design major, who displayed clothing she had designed and sewn to serve as her death wardrobe at her wake and when she is placed in the earth. She obviously wanted to depart as a blazing star, having fashioned a wardrobe vibrating with shimmering reds, yellows and purples, with a touch of black here and there.

At the conclusion of her presentation, I asked Shelby if she had given any thought to designing clothes for young women at death's door. "No, I haven't she said, but what an interesting idea." Once again, facing death had resulted in an opportunity to embark on a new path in life.

Without question, the most emotionally healing and heart opening class assignment for the students calls for the initiation of a dialogue with their parents centered on thoughts and feelings about death and dying. Healing in the sense of emotions being brought to the surface and dealt with in such a manner as to disassemble fences and walls erected largely as a result of perceived or actual hurts experienced not too uncommonly in the course of family life. Such wounds often result in the ossification of family dynamics, eventually turning into barriers serving to keep loved ones from opening themselves up to those who can hurt them very deeply—those whom they love and are closest to.

There is of magic in the air waiting to be realized when we speak to loved ones about death and dying. It is as if heart pierced by arrow, resulting not in a flood of blood, but in emotional vulnerability and an openness of such scope and depth that the involved parties are afforded an opportunity to erect a bridge over troubled waters, allowing the forces of forgiveness, love and compassion to soften hardened hearts. Seeds of grace sowed within each other in the realm of the now, in this lifetime, in the form of an awareness of the preciousness of life that is an unparalleled final gift to share with those whom we love and cherish.

It always occurs that at some point during our first class meeting a student will ask, what happens after you die? My answer has not changed over the years. It is, in the true spirit of the course: What happens after we live, after we learn how to let go of the "death" within us, that which suppresses the life force, the cosmic energy embodied in our beings, freeing us to be fully alive?

Planting Seeds

Teachers often plant seeds of awareness and awakening in their students, yet are never certain as to whether or not these seeds have taken root, to germinate at some point in the future. For the seed to burst from dormancy and take root, in the process of which a foundation is established for a life beyond that of present existence, one must be willing to let go an aspect of self that is in need of being cast off in order for a new self to emerge.

> **Subject:** *I'm a former student of yours . . .*
> **Date:** *Thursday, May 25, 2006 4:32 PM*
> **From:** *chris . . .*
> **To:** *<lsilverstein@colum.edu>*

Dear Louis,

My name is Chris . . . , and I am a former student of yours from a few years back. I took your Peace Studies class and another one I believe was called Education, Culture, and Society. Please forgive me if I got the name wrong of the latter.

I wanted to write you a letter sincerely expressing my heartfelt gratitude to you for planting some vital seeds in my heart and my conscience during the time you were my teacher. I believe that during the Peace Studies class I did not do much to stick out as a student, so I am not so sure if you will remember me, but the essence of that course had a profound effect on me and the direction that my life has taken since.

Your Peace Studies class sparked in me serious inquiry into the fundamental nature of human beings, and our purpose here on Earth, and the myriad ethical challenges we face as a civilization at the dawn of the 21st Century. This inquiry took root in a major search for meaning and spirituality that culminated in me ordaining as a Zen Buddhist monk last month in Dalat,

Vietnam, where I was living and working as an English teacher for the past year.

I do not remember if we touched specifically upon Buddhist wisdom in your courses, but I naturally drifted towards this profound system of philosophy and practice after some of the seeds planted by your Peace Studies course came to grow and bear fruit after I graduated from Columbia in 2004. I hope you know deeply in your heart your ability to inspire within your students (even the most seemingly apathetic of ones, like myself) such wonderful curiosity about ourselves and the world around us, about our love, our interdependence, our horrors and our ignorance, and ultimately, our total, perfect, all-embracing enlightenment. Your ability as an educator, as a vehicle of wisdom and positivity, is priceless in this world of samsara. Thank you.

Sincerely,

Chris

(Dharma name: Thich Thien Tri)

A Course Evaluation

At the end of the semester, each student is asked to write a course evaluation, the author of which is to remain anonymous. Beginning with the first time this class was offered and running through each succeeding term, a common sentiment has been expressed, threading the hundreds of evaluations into a tapestry woven of compassion and love within the context of reaching out to imperfect human beings and facing life's endings as opportunities for the renewal of our journey on earth.

By asking my students to focus not on giving thought to meeting those we love at some indefinite time on the other side, but to reflect upon meeting each other mindfully in the present moment, they are challenged to be brave enough to live in here and now. What follows are representative samples of how this challenge was met by students who chose to reach out to their loved ones, not in the absence of fear of rejection, but in its presence, which is what courage is all about.

"Louis's class prepares a person for things in life that we seldom think about, but are so important. What if today was our last day on earth? Have we said all we needed to say to the people we love? Have we given forgiveness to those seeking it? After taking this class I tried to make amends with two people in my life, one a past lover who I was hurt by and a young girl who unknowingly hurt me. I asked them both for their forgiveness, even though they did me wrong. If I die tomorrow, I want to leave with dignity, and a clear conscience."

*   *   *

"I have never been faced with having to consider needing reconciliation. What I mean is that I've never seen someone on his or her hospital bed trying to make peace with someone else. But our classroom discussion made me think about the people in my life who I have loved or touched personally. As death nears, people often realize some things feel unfinished or incomplete. It made me think about my family, although, I'm really close to my mom, I think I would need to apologize to my dad and his part of the family because I have shielded them out of my life for years. Although, I hate this battle I have with them, I feel I would need to get things off my chest, in order to make peace for my self. Our class opened up my mind, to the point, where this coming Father's Day, I am going to speak with my dad and declare peace between him and I, because if I would leave here sooner than next week, I would want to clear the air between us."

*   *   *

"After discussing the importance of realizing that only the present moment is certain, and that now is the time to say what needs to be said to our loved ones, I went home and told my parents what I would want them to know when their life comes to an end. 'Mom and dad, I have something of importance to share with you. I want to thank you for being my parents. I want to tell you how grateful I am for the life you have given me. I want you to know I love you.'

We made the most beautiful life music in that night in my home. My parents and I expressed and felt love and compassion for our each other in a way that hasn't occurred since I was a child."

*   *   *

"I know there is no guaranteed happy ending to a life. I know that the world can be a coarse, brutal, cruel and despairing place. After taking this class and having you as a teacher, I know I can go beyond the rejection I've experienced in my life. I know that if I want to die in peace, I need to take the risk of being hurt by those I care about if I am to be open to receive whatever love life has in store for me. I know I need to let go of a lot if there is to be room in me for life's joys to find a home within. Thank you for touching me in the way that you have. I love you. You are a great teacher. You've changed my life."

Lesson From Another Class

During the summer semester, I teach two classes: "Death and Dying" and "Social Problems In American Society." During a class discussion in the Social Problems course, I asked each of my students this question. If they were to be granted a super power what would they choose? Needless to say, the responses were diverse in terms of specifics, but with rare exception the choices centered on the self at play in the exterior world. Ranging from an ability to see through walls, to fly through the sky, to make gold out of clay, they wanted to be able to do things that would make them more powerful, or bring them riches in the material world.

When a student in the class asked me what super power I would want to possess, being their teacher I granted myself the prerogative to choose two. In response to a question as to what he thought of western civilization, Gandhi replied, "I think it would be a good idea." Surely, should we be asked on our deathbed whether or not our walk on earth was a civilizing influence, an answer other than, it would have been a good idea, is to be desired.

So my first choice would be to sow seeds of justice wherever there is injustice and seeds of beauty wherever there is ugliness. In essence, to do unto others as I would want others to do unto me. Yes, let us remember and pay due respect to the dead. However, let us not forget that the living are more in need of a helping hand than the departed.

Second, at the deepest core of my being to open myself up as widely and deeply as humanly possible in order to take in and absorb the boundless and uplifting love that my wife and children offer unto me.

Surely, to introduce such life forces into the curriculum in informed, creative and disciplined ways would mean the end of modes of schooling that suppress life's breath, which is love, from being unleashed as an integral aspect of the educational process. If the pursuit of knowledge and skills were to be infused with love, then what we call education, what and how we learn, would be suitable for human habitation whether it be applied to learning about living or learning about dying.

Practices To Live Our Dying

We all have a need
to dissolve, shape, shift,
and become One
with a larger truth . . .
you both celebrate
birth just before spring . . .
when winter wants
to dissolve
and give herself
to a new cycle of growth . . .
the ice wants
to melt and return
to the ocean . . .
water gives up
its identity and seeps into the ground
to merge with the soil . . .
it rises into the air to encircle the globe
and return as rain . . .

the seed begins a dance of self-undoing . . .
she gives up
the shell that made her
a seed
so she can become a sprout . . .
birth requires sacrifice . . .
the old must die
for the new
to discover herself . . .
this season knows
what other seasons question . . .
it knows the touch
of The Great Mystical Oneness
that transcends
physical form
time and
space
to find Union.

Hazel Aura G

To Rebel Against Being Among The Living Dead

A DREAM.
I see elderly women and men, living in an institutionalized setting, a caretaker facility,

all shook up. A pleasure attacker has been on the loose, inflicting random acts of pleasure on unsuspecting residents, their bodies experiencing paroxysms of rapturous delight.

Dogs are brought in to sniff out the criminal giver of such thrills, but to no avail. As soon as the dogs sniff pleasure to be close by, they swoon, fall down on the ground, and eagerly await the pleasure attacker, for they, too, are pleasure starved, having been placed on a pleasure diet by their masters who have a low pleasure tolerance like all mad people.

The elderly ask, what are we to do? The keepers guarding the institution tell them to pray and ask for divine protection from unbridled pleasure lest they wish to be denied entrance to the heaven of the cross of pain. And so they pray, but this, too, is to no avail, for that very night two patients are made to endure pleasure attacks. The authorities throw up their hands, decide to close down the residence, and move its inhabitants to a maximum-security pleasure protection facility to better ensure that life may be lived in a normal fashion where pleasure is managed and a hypnotic stupor of sitting and staring at emptiness is enforced as the norm for the elderly and the dying.

In the June 27, 2002 issue of *The Week* magazine, a story appeared centered on the sexual relationship between two residents of a senior center—a ninety-five year old man and his eighty-two old girlfriend. Horrified by catching the woman performing oral sex on his father, the son had his father removed from the facility, resulting in severe depression being experienced by the two lovers.

This story is akin to what Paula E told my Death & Dying about walking into the room of a terminal ill patient to find he and his wife making whoopee, and going into another room on a different day to find a terminal ill patient with his night gown over his head engaged in a fervent act of self-pleasuring.

The cultural picture we are asked to accept as the norm, to buy into as the way to go, is that dying and pain go together like a horse and carriage Without a doubt there is much truth to such a portrayal of what dying can be all about. However, just as is the case in our lives prior to facing our demise, the presence of pain does not exclude the possibility of pleasure coming through the door and pushing the pain aside, if only for a few moments, so that life can be enjoyed and not merely endured.

Why not create a revised paradigm of the dying experience in which the introduction of pleasure to whatever degree possible is afforded as high a priority as is the reduction of pain? Be it drink or drugs. Be it massage, self-pleasuring, sex or other forms of bringing joy to the body. Be it a bed by the endless sea or on a meadow under an endless sky. Be it images of Christ, or Mary, or Buddha, or the Mona Lisa. Be it listening to the Grateful Dead, or Miles Davis, or Arthur Rubenstein, or Bob Dylan, or Ella Fitzgerald, or Luciano Pavarotti, or Phoenix Rising. Be it . . . Why not unleash the human possibility for taking the dying into heaven while still alive?

Being With The Dying

As we were preparing for the birth of our first child, I shared with my wife the insecurity I was feeling about what I should say and do to support her during the delivery. This being her first birthing, Paula responded that as far as specifics were concerned, she wasn't certain about what would be required of me during this monumental event in our lives. However, there was one thing she was certain of. Namely, the center of attention in the birthing room was to be her, and that any agenda items of mine about what I would like for her to do and what I should want to do during the birthing were not to be brought into the room. My role was to be there for her, to listen and do my very best to allow her to express her feelings, and to fulfill her needs and desires. In sum and essence, to be totally committed to being Paula's caregiver, to be there for her.

What is demanded of us and needed by those whose lives are ending? Which face of ours should we wear and what should we say and do in the presence of those who are dying? To offer sympathy well beyond what the circumstances call for, or to deny the reality of what is transpiring when in the presence of death, is most likely attributable to the fact that the dying serve as a mirror for us to face our relationship to our mortality. Looking into their eyes we see ourselves, and are confronted with the reality that we too will die, a realization serving to bring forth in our guts as well as our minds the fears and anxieties we possess about the ending of our lives, of no longer being with our loved ones, about no longer being here.

What then is the primary challenge when being with the dying? It is to center our attention and devote ourselves to attending to the feelings, needs and desires of he or she who is to about to die. Our task is to neither advise nor instruct, but to ask and listen. To be, once again, a compassionate and engaged caregiver.

Three Wishes

Knowing and accepting that death is inevitable and can happen at any time in our lives affords us the opportunity to focus on what is most precious to us, to take action to enhance the way we live, which, in turn, will enhance the way we die. Loretta Downs, a guest speaker in my class on a number of occasions, has my students undertake the following exercise in order to have them realize the importance and opportunity of living our dying.

She requests of them to assume that they have, at most, six months to live, and to write down three things they would want to do. After the students have placed their words on paper, Loretta asks them to respond to two questions. How many of you would want to spend more time with your loved ones? How many of you would want to travel? Virtually all hands are raised.

Of course, once we acknowledge our desire to spend more time with our loved ones, we realize that there is seemingly never enough time to do so in light of all the duties and responsibilities our lives are occupied with. We are faced with the fact that unless we consciously prioritize how we are going about spending our lives, the point in time will arrive when time to be with our loved ones will no longer be possible due to life's endings. Given such a reality, we are given the opportunity to choose to live in the present moment. To be with our loved ones not before the end of our lives, but before the end of the day.

To be certain, let us fulfill our travel desires, be it to places near and far, wherever in the gardens of the physical world we wish to experience having been there for the myriad reasons and needs humans have always yearned to tread in different places on the planet. However, let us remember that our world is composed of being with, that is, in relationship to others, as well as of being away.

As for the third wish, student responses are varied in nature, ranging from creating a memorable work of art, literary, visual, craft or performance, to be treasured long after ones demise, to contributing in some substantial manner to make the world a better place for ones children. In essence, to live on in the minds and hearts of others by virtue of good deeds undertaken while alive that will contribute to the dying out of the dominant cultural mindset of I came, I saw, I conquered, long in need of being supplanted by one in service to the forces of light. I came. I saw. I shared.

Epitaph

It is a cold and wintry Sunday morning. Paula has finished savoring her café con leche as she read and sent her email, and I have completed my morning routine of yoga and meditation. Sitting at the kitchen table facing each other, shortly to take on the task and challenge of writing our epitaphs, we are reflecting upon what we wish our final words to be, the essence of ourselves that we wish to conjure up in the thoughts of those we leave behind.

Why are we doing this? Haven't we been responsible enough, completing estate planning documents, living wills, powers of attorney, discussing with our children our wishes should we require care as we age as well as informing them of what is to be done with our ashes? Is there really a need, once again, for us to confront our mortality? Have we not cried enough for those who have gone before us? Have we not already experienced to an almost unbearable degree the deep sorrow of knowing that one day we will not be able to hold each other in our arms and feel the tender and loving warmth of our lover's body?

The answer, of course, is yes. Death and dying are beyond why. The losses experienced during these passages, of body, mind, status, purpose, meaning, can be mitigated, if not offset, to an appreciable degree by knowing that our loved ones will keep us alive in their memories and hearts. Leave here as you hopefully lived it—being true to yourself. Seize the opportunity to tell the world of your track marks, the traces of yourself you wish to be remembered by.

So, it is time for me to compose my epitaph, a few words that will be my final message to the world. The truth is, as my life experience has taught me, who knows if there will be a tomorrow to take up this task?

"Loving and devoted husband of Paula Inocencia Cofresi-Silverstein and father of Ana Rebeca Cofresi-Silverstein and Ben Rafael Cofresi-Silverstein. His presence graced all who knew him. Till we meet again. Good traveling in heaven."

Beyond Fear

Choose a setting, either indoors or outdoors, which is conducive to making you feel relaxed. Sit or lie down whichever makes you feel more comfortable. Close your eyes. Become aware of your breathing. Breathe in slowly and deeply to the count of five. Hold your breath to the count of five. Exhale slowly to the count of five. Center yourself as you give full attention to your breathing. Repeat this pattern for two or three minutes.

With your eyes remaining closed, see yourself as you are now. Now, decade after decade see yourself growing older until you are very old to the point in time of your dying. See yourself dying.

Allow whatever fears you have about growing old and dying to come to the surface, be they the widely held fears of becoming ill, being in pain, witnessing he deterioration of your body, losing loved ones, being alone, or fears of any other nature or kind that cause you to feel apprehensive and distressed.

One by one, let go of each fear by using your breath to exhale it out of your mind and heart so that it is no longer attached to your consciousness.

Focus your attention on your breathing.

Inhale the life force.

Exhale the fear of becoming ill.

Inhale the life force.

Exhale the fear of being in pain.

Inhale the life force.

Exhale the fear of witnessing the deterioration of your body.

Inhale the life force.

Exhale the fear of losing loved ones.

Inhale the life force.

Exhale the fear of being alone.

Inhale the life force.

Let feelings of well-being and being with loved ones fill your heart and mind.

Slowly open your eyes and go on with your life.

President Franklin D. Roosevelt spoke the truth when, during the Great Depression, he reminded his fellow Americans enmeshed in dealing with the end of a world they had thought would last forever: "We have nothing to fear, but fear itself."

Remember that you are not your body. Your essence knows neither illness nor pain nor deterioration.

Remember also that as you live, so shall you die. Love well while alive and your loved ones will be with you beyond this life. Those here now and those who have preceded you.

Cry A River

You will die. How sad. Cry. All those you love will die. Weep. You will experience the loss of everybody and everything your life is centered on. Howl. You will hurt and be hurt by others. Moan. Someday even the Earth, as we have known it, will die. Cry like a river. Broken in mind body and spirit, the burden of your grief weighs you down until you fall to the ground unable to get up. Days, weeks, months, perhaps even years will go by and yet you lay where you first placed your body. Will I ever get up you wonder? Will my tears ever cease you ask of yourself?

Yet, the truth is all that exists will pass. Good will pass. Bad will pass. Happiness will pass. Sorrow will pass. Joy will pass. Grief will pass. The day will come when you can cry no more; when you cannot gaze upon flowers, sky, sun, moon, the smile of a child, the eyes of others; when hands outstretched to help lift you up cannot be grasped; when the voices of your spouse and children will be echoes in the wind; when you will be dust carried by wind.

So, cry. Do not hold back. Cry. Let it all hang out. Cry. Let yourself go. Cry. Let go of all the fear, guilt, disappointment, pain, misery and sorrow within you. Cry. Yes, cry like an overflowing river so that its waters may carry you into the life that you have left to live.

Gratitude

Breathe slowly and deeply. See yourself resting comfortably in your bed about to go to sleep. Close your eyes and allow your thoughts to reflect upon all that you are grateful for, all that which has contributed to making you the person who you are and to the life that you are living today. Without focusing on any individual person or experience, speak these words to all those to whom you owe gratitude, repeating them three times.

I am grateful for what life has brought me and for what I have made of my life. I know that each and every experience and each and every person has been the clay of my life, serving to shape who I am.

Once the repetitions are completed, be still, allowing yourself to breathe in and be nourished by what you are feeling at that moment.

Valuing Our Time

> . . . our days on the earth are as a shadow
>
> *I Chronicles*

Life is short. Our lives go by so fast. We grow old and wonder where the time went. Time is precious. Value time for the treasure it truly is. Who knows how many years, months, weeks, days, minutes or seconds are left in our lives or in the lives of our loved ones? The future is a possibility, not a certainty. What is the lesson to be learned here? Make each and every flash of your life count. It is these moments that make up a life. It is during these moments that we gift the world with our lives.

At the beginning of each day write down three gifts of life's treasures—love, compassion, caring, justice, peace, joy—you wish to share with the world before you go to sleep that night. Carry this list with you as you go about the day to serve as a reminder of whether or not you have fulfilled your promises of the day to the world.

Repeat this exercise for as long as it takes to incorporate the sharing of these gifts into your life as a daily practice. Do so and your life will be one to be treasured, the value of which having no limits both during your time here and after you have departed.

Ethical Will

A life has a beginning and an end. To die is as much of what a life is about as it is to be born. Those who are dying, knowing time is a precious commodity, wish to derive as much value as possible from each moment, each day. As we face and struggle with the inevitability of death, we are also afforded the opportunity to complete and close our life's journey in as meaningful and purposeful manner as is possible through our efforts and the efforts of those who we have been in close relationship with.

How do we wish to be remembered? What knowledge, thoughts, ideas, values, beliefs, memories, teachings and blessings do we wish to leave with those who will be left behind? Sharing with our loved ones the why(s) and how(s) of our lives, in essence, our life story and philosophy, as well as informing them about what principles, values, and beliefs we wish them to consider as life guides can make separation and dying somewhat easier.

Yes, there is much truth to those who say this reality is a material world. In accordance with such a belief, more often than not, those who choose to have a will written or a trust established focus on their property and other material possessions. However, just as what a really want is a father's presence much more than his presents, we will be remembered not so much by what we bought, but by what we brought, why(s) and how(s) of the life we lived.

The writing of an ethical will, as is the case with a more traditional will, can be a challenging, perhaps even formidable task, because it requires of us to accept our mortality, to face death absent of any semblance of denial, and see it as an opportunity to allow our life story to continue on beyond our passing. Denial of death is one of the more powerful forces in our consciousness. Yet, the acceptance of death can allow us to see beyond the veils that shield us from viewing what has always been there if we were to only open our eyes—the foundation on which our lives have been built. An ethical will can be a key to immortality because such a gift presents us with the opportunity to live on in the hearts and minds of those whom we loved and shared our lives with.

What is written is a matter of individual choice. Perhaps, however, beginning with words that open hearts and minds to take in what we wish to convey in a most thoughtful and heartfelt manner would be in harmony with the spirit of the will. A suggestion: "I ask you to forgive me for all the angry moments I have shown you and to pardon me for whatever pain, despair and shame that I have caused you. I ask you to cherish me for all the happy moments I have shared with you and to cherish whatever joy and pleasure, meaning and fulfillment I have brought to you. Know that I shall always love you, always be with you, and that we shall meet again."

Taking the time to reflect upon the course of our lives in a thoughtful manner and sharing such knowledge in the form of a written, audio or visual testimonial also can serve as a gift to ourselves. It allows us to give closure to what has passed as well as serve to inform us as to what we wish to say and do during the time we have left.

Waiting for the deathbed to compose such a legacy for our loved ones centered on what was and is truly important to us during the of days our lives assumes that we will be in control of our capacities and in a functioning state of mind at that time, an assumption that might prove to be untrue as well as true. Waiting also increases the possibility of letting others tell you what they learned from having you in their lives might never occur. Waiting is for those who know with certainty that tomorrow will come and not even the gods and goddesses know that.

Waiting until we are dying to share intimacy of such a nature diminishes the life we are living in the present moment, depriving our loved ones of the opportunity to know us in ways that can impact their lives in a profound manner. Intimacy feeds the heart, which, in turn, nourishes the souls of both those who give as well as those who receive.

Transition

Fill an empty glass with water. Notice that what was once empty is now full. Now fill a teaspoon with sugar. Notice the presence of the sugar. Place the sugar into the glass of water. Stir the sugar. Notice that the sugar has dissolved and appears to no longer have any presence. Yet, what appears to be is not reality. What has changed is the form of the sugar, its separateness. Sugar, having surrendered its individuality, and water have become one.

Yet, had sugar, notwithstanding the fact that its time had come to submit to its destiny, been determined not to soften itself, not to melt and merge into that which was greater than itself, resolving to retain its hardness and rigidity, the outcome would have been the same—sugar and water as one. However, the transition would have been burdened with fear and anger, rather than with acceptance and peacefulness.

Breathe deeply. Allow your body to relax and your mind to focus solely on your breathing. See yourself at your place of dying. However, instead of being in a deathbed, you are lying in a meadow of wildflowers, or on the shore by the ocean, encircled by your loved ones. In the background you hear a harp playing the most heavenly and rapturous of sounds.

Continue to breathe as you fix your attention on either the seemingly endless sky or ocean. Allow yourself to drift into the sky or ocean, slowly merging into that which is greater than you, becoming one with the infinite. Neither borders nor limits are known to you at this time. Rest in this place of eternity and serenity for a few minutes, allowing yourself to experience what dying can be should you choose such a pathway to life's endings.

Loving Kindness

Centering, a stilling of the self, is not a means of going where we want to go. Rather, it places us in a state of higher consciousness and thus fosters a favorable atmosphere for the development of the deeper awareness to which our spiritual nature is attracted. The purpose of centering is to facilitate the process of inner transformation, the base from which to heal and transform others and the world around us.

Centering is a way of becoming aware of the reality in which we are immersed. Rarely do we give thought to the air that we breathe, yet it is in us and around us always. Thoughts are like ocean waves. As a wave rises and falls, we see only its singularity, its separateness. Viewing what we deem reality through such a lens, if we were waves, we would think we are waves, when, in reality, the truth is that each wave is inseparable from ocean. There is no separation between waves and ocean save in our mind's eye. It is when a wave recedes to merge with its source that we clearly see with full awareness its seeming beginning and apparent end resides as an unity in an infinite and eternal ocean.

Mind is of the same nature. Based on the principle that a mind is a terrible thing to waste, it is busy as a bee, thinking all the time as if a mind at rest were a betrayal of what it is to be human. However, when the mind stops acting like a chattering monkey, it returns to its source and becomes still.

And what is the nature of this source? If we were to peel an onion one layer after another until there were no layers left, we would apparently see nothing at its center. Yes, despite appearances, it is from that ostensible nothingness that life originates, be it a wave, an onion or oneself. Centering allows us to experience that seeming nothingness, the stillness where the universes and the self are one and the same—the source of the life force.

Sit comfortably with your back relatively upright so that you have a sense of poise and dignity. Breathe deeply as you center yourself. Starting from the feet and working up to your head, notice the physical sensations in your body. Where there is tension or stress, breathe into that part of your body in order to relax it. Bring your attention more fully to your breathing. Breathe in slowly to the count of five. Hold your breath to the count of five. Exhale slowly to the count of five. Repeat until you feel fully relaxed.

Turning within, send kindness, compassion and peace to yourself for your own well being. With each in-breath speak to your heart, saying, "May I be free from suffering. May I be at peace." On each out-breath, say, "May I be free from suffering. May I be at peace." Repeat these words slowly and gently with each in-breath and each out-breath, deepening the nurturing warmth of relating to yourself with loving kindness, compassion and peace.

Now focus your mind on a loved one who is gravely ill or dying. Visualize this beloved in your heart, and with each in-breath, speak these words. "May you be free from suffering." With each out-breath, "May you be at peace." Repeat these words as long as the spirit to do so moves you.

Take In The Beauty

While walking on the streets of life, I have a tendency to look down at life's garbage, literally as well as symbolically, in need of being picked up and dealt with. A state of mind not inherently conducive to giving attention to the beautiful along the way, and that can lead to being "down," sad or even depressed as an integral part of the way we go about our lives.

To my good fortune I share my life with a Latina born on the tropical island of Puerto Rico and taught by culture and her mother to see the beauty in life. She, in turn, has moved me in the direction of setting my eyes upon the beautiful. As a result of doing so, I experience an elevated energy state, providing me with the necessary sustenance to encounter what is awry with me and the world at-large in such a manner as to deal with life's troubles and challenges in a much more effective way. To put it another way, with my head held high, I am able to keep on walking through the valley of the shadow of death because I keep my sight on the light shining through the darkness in the distance.

Yes, we will feel sorrow as we approach the end of our lives. Feeling sad is a legitimate feeling, not to be denied. So, take the time to see flowers, trees, sea, sky, children's faces, dancers, musicians and lovers. Breathe in deeply that which is beautiful on the earthly plane so that your spirits may be lifted.

To be sure, beauty is not a panacea, a cure-all for that everything that is not going our way. However, it is many steps above aspirin for taking on life's worries and difficulties. Beauty is not only a great shoulder to lean on when the going gets rough. It intoxicates the soul, filling it up with the necessary sustenance to help us make it through the days and nights of our lives with hope in our hearts and a vision of human possibility in our minds.

A Life Filled Body

Let your body live before it dies. A body satiated to its core with the joys and pleasures of life is more willing to surrender to death's call, for it has no regrets about not having taking full advantage of having been alive. Ecstasy is at the essence of the world, ever-present beyond the veil shielded by ordinary existence. Yet, many have lost the capacity to fully surrender to bliss, flitting from one pleasureful experience to another, never taking pleasure in deeply, never feeling filled up with pleasure, always hungry for more. To remedy this, a journey of transformation needs to be undertaken. Sensual pleasures cultivated and refined through rapturous experience, revealing a path into transcendental bliss.

Visualizing a scene of desired sensuality allow your body to be receptive to pleasure of such a nature as to transcend time and space guiding yourself as follows. I slowly breathe in the swirling crimson vortex of sensual energy, seeing and feeling it flowing to my heart, nourishing my love center with its vital force. I allow myself to relish in this state of being for a few minutes. The vortex begins to flow upward through my spine, releasing all the holy serpentine power Eve bestowed upon Adam. I allow myself to relish in this state of being for a few minutes. The vortex continues to move upward until it rests in the center of my brain, bathing it with a higher wisdom than reason alone can ever know. I allow myself to relish in this state of being for a few minutes.

I am so alive.

At The Source

It is one of those blessed summer days that serve as a time of passage between summer and fall. I am sitting on a weathered gray wooden bench in my backyard. Scurrying all about me are squirrels, chipmunks, birds and bees in a garden of elm, cottonwood, ash and evergreen trees, roses, marigolds, brown eyed susan, coneflower, hosta, lily, cosmos, sage, ivy, peony, honeysuckle and moss. Placed throughout the garden are Buddhas, Quan Yins and other sacred objects.

I am on a journey guided by my long-time friend ganja. My defenses are down, bridges to where I am are in place, and mind and heart are wide open in a state of receptivity. Closing my eyes while breathing fully and deeply, my body sways gently back and forth as if I were prairie grass blowing in the wind. The clouds blocking my consciousness from seeing clearly dissipate as I find myself swimming in a river of universal love flowing out from within me, the source of which is the loving heart I have worked hard over the years to cultivate as such.

Place yourself in a natural setting of calmness and beauty. Close your eyes. Breathe slowly and deeply as you visualize a luminous lotus flower of exquisite beauty arising out of mud filled pond just a few feet from you. Repeat, for a few moments, as if it were a mantra, these words: "Take me to the love." Let go of all that is holding you back from taking wing and returning to the source from which you came, which, for all sentient beings, is the same for you as it is for me—universal love.

Bring this love back with you as you return your attention back to being in the garden. Know that this love is always flowing within you to share with whomever is in need, the dying as well as the living, including yourself.

Healing

Your body is not so much fixed as a flowing stream of atoms and electrons in constant motion. Beneath the physical surface, you are wave coming to shore and then receding into ocean. If you were to view your body at its essence, it is an oscillating and pulsating pattern of light and energy. At all stages of life, including when we are dying, a body is more a work in progress than a fixed and solid tomb in the making, more clay than a final work.

Breathe deeply as you center yourself. Visualize divine and loving light flowing from your heart out through your hands. Sacred hands, instruments of divine love, tools of the soul to be used to express the gifts of spirit. Sitting closely to the person who is dying, take his or her hands in yours, and with eyes filled with compassion and care look into his or her eyes, the mirrors into our souls, as your loving touch fills the dying person with the knowledge and feeling of being cherished.

See in your mind's eye above the dying person a vibrating vortex composed of rose colored light representing self-love and self-worth, white light representing purity, black light representing eternal grace and harmony, and indigo light representing the gift of being divine. Now see all of his or her emotional suffering, be it based in pain, guilt, resentment, anger, disillusionment or despair dissolve into the vortex as they are replaced by feelings of acceptance, surrender and peace.

A Final Gift

Each death is unique to the person undergoing that experience. Yet, death is not an individual act. The dying person is a performer in a drama that will be observed by others and participated in by others. Like the last will and testament we leave upon our deaths that materially benefits those who survive us, we also leave to others a legacy of how we have experienced our own death.

What is the "final gift" that we would want to give to ourselves and our loved ones at the time of our passing keeping in mind that the most often spoken words on a death bed are, "Forgive me. I love you." Why not give such to give to ourselves and our loved ones now.

As my brother Joe lay dying, what he wanted most was to be relieved of pain and anxiety, a task we left to the attending physician to be effectuated by means of morphine and other drugs, and to be held as if there were to be no tomorrow, which for him was an immediate reality. Our need for touch is as much a necessity for the living as well as it is for the dying, because without it the life spirit within us withers. There is no better way to let others we know and cherish that they exist in a meaningful way for us and that we care for them deeply than to embrace them as if these moments would be the last time we held each other in our arms.

Center yourself as you breathe deeply. Allow your attention to be focused on your heart as you feel the love flowing within it. Now see your heart opening up as a red river of love streams from it into your arms and hands. Release the river of love from your arms and hands allowing it to envelop your loved one. Remember to breathe. Stay with this embrace for as long as it is genuine. Melt into each other's arms.

Tell each other, "I ask you to forgive me for all the angry moments I have shown you and to pardon me for whatever pain, despair and shame that I have caused you. I ask you to cherish me for all the happy moments I have shared with you and to cherish whatever joy and pleasure, meaning and fulfillment I have brought to you. Know that I shall always love you, always be with you, and that we shall meet again."

Merging

Ideally, this visualization would take place while sitting by the ocean under a clear blue sky as the sun is setting. However, viewing images of sunset, ocean and sky captured in a book, photograph, painting, television screen or on a computer monitor would suffice.

Close your eyes and become aware of your breathing. Count to five slowly as you breathe in. Hold your breath to the count of five. Exhale to the count of five. Hold your exhalation to the count of five. Should a thought or image come to mind, do not fret. It is not a problem. Just continue to focus your attention on your breathing and whatever comes to mind will drift away.

Repeat this centering process until you feel completely relaxed. Continue to engage in conscious breathing. As you open your eyes fix your attention on the setting sun, ocean and sky in this order and say the following words over and over.

I am greater than my body.

I am sunrise.

I am sunset.

I am wave merging with ocean.
I am endless sky.
I am greater than my body.

Rebirth

Reincarnation is usually thought of in relation to the end of a physical life in this existence on the earthly plane, and a return in another life form as a manifestation of the cycle of a soul. However, for the purpose of this exercise, focus on the opportunity and challenge to reincarnate in this lifetime, not in a new body, but, rather, in the same body, but at a higher and more fulfilled state of being.

How is this to be accomplished? By reflecting upon what you need to let go of and sow in the empty space now within you as result of having discarded that which has kept you mired in muck, be it in the form of hatred, anger, grievance, resentment, regret, anger, guilt, or whatever else has kept you imprisoned as one of the living dead; that is, being less of the person that you are capable of revealing, not allowing the great soul that you are to manifest in its wholeness.

By eliminating that part of yourself which is lifeless, an area is created within you for the life force to enter, liberating from its encasement the seed of life within you that has been waiting to sprout so that change and healing can take place, allowing yourself to live in the now and to experience what lies before you.

Is such a death and rebirth possible?

Close your eyes and visualize yourself as being a lotus representing purity and spiritual power. Rooted in the mud but blossoming above the water, completely unsullied by the muck, the lotus symbolizes both the possibility of transformation and spiritual perfection.

Scan your thoughts, values, beliefs and actions, looking for the life's hurts and scars, resulting in weeds of a noxious nature having been planted within you. Ask yourself, in the realm of my beliefs, values, thoughts and behaviors, what do I need to "die," to let go of, in order to be more fully alive, to be present in the moment? Why have I not allowed these hindrances and blockages to pass on? What role(s) does each play in being who I am that if let go of would result in my facing a life challenge of momentous importance? The challenge I face being to allow life's breath to enter me in such a way that the stunted self I have accepted as my station in life to be discarded, replaced by a fully alive person. What do I need to do to dispose of such negative influences in my life? How might I learn to accomplish such goal?

After having identified these negative aspects of self, ask yourself, in the realm of my beliefs, values, thoughts and behaviors, what do I need to give birth to in order to live life more fully? Why have I not allowed these seeds/possibilities to be manifested in my life? How would my life be for the better if these were birthed? What do I need to do to incorporate such positive influences into my life? How might I learn to accomplish such a goal?

Now comes the hard part. Doing the necessary work on self to incorporate such realizations into ones daily life, a challenge stated so well in a Greenpeace motto: "Do not tell me what you believe. Tell me what you do each day, and I will tell you what you believe." Whether it be by means of therapy—body and mind, meditation, visualization, prayer, or a combination thereof depends on your individual needs and what will work best for you. The task ahead is to take the first step on the thousand mile journey, for the initial step is the hardest in that it takes courage of high order to admit to having been the one who has hurt others as well as having been the one who has experienced being hurt.

Dying, Death and Enlightenment

WHY DO GOOD people suffer? Why do good people die? Students or audience members at my presentations on the subject of death and dying often ask me such questions. My answer is a simple one. It is akin to asking why good people even have to die? Good people suffer and die for the very same reason bad people do? Not due to of a lack of good works, or from having to burn off karma, but because suffering and dying, as is the case with joy and living, are included in the price we pay for being alive. Yes, good people will suffer and die because suffering and death are always present in the realm of human existence. In the case of suffering, parceled out on a random basis. In the case of death, the fate of all.

Understanding brings us knowledge, not necessarily wisdom or enlightenment. Might there be questions for which there are no answers notwithstanding the human need for an explanation to all inquiries on the subject of what living and dying are all about? Is it not possible that the incomprehensible is at work here? Might life at its very core not be a puzzle so much waiting to be solved, but a mystery to accept as the way it is and to get on with living our lives?

Does it not make sense to allow the wisdom teachings of those who know what is most important about living to instruct us as to how best to separate the wheat from the chaff from life's callings, and to serve as guidelines for living life in such a manner that when the time of our dying comes, we can surrender to its call with acceptance? A basic teaching of these life guides is that a good death is knowing that we have lived life fully, and to incorporate giving and receiving love and compassion as an essential part of our daily life practice

Who are these wise souls? Quite simply, those who have lived their lives and, from the vantage point of facing life's endings, speak words to be heard again and again during our dying days. What are these transformative spoken words? "Forgive me. I love you."

The life lesson to be learned becomes quite clear. To give life to these words and what each represents in the now, during the course of everyday existence, and not wait until we die to speak and hear such magic that heals body, mind and soul. To, remember what we have already learned. Bring flowers to the living as well as to the dying.

Have we led our lives in such a manner as to require little need at the time of life's endings to offer unto others forgiveness, for love not given, for care not provided? Have we led lives of being compassionate and making love to self, others, the earth and all its life forms to the extent that all know that they have been loved? Have we led lives of such a nature that when we are on our deathbed, there will be little need to say "I love you" other than as a reminder and as a final gift?

However, should there be need for an exchange of forgiveness, or to tell others of our love for them, do not bewail what has not occurred until now. No feelings or expressions of guilt are necessary. We all do the best we can. Always remember all of us are broken in some way to let the light to come in.

So what is enlightenment? It is, as those closest to the heaven beyond this reality inform us, a quest. It is a practice, not a body of knowledge. It is a path, not a destination. It is not to find heaven, but, as spiritual beings created out of divine substance, to make a heaven wherever and whatever we are, be it here or there. It is in the doing. It is in the living.

A Closing Is Not An Ending

AMONG THE LEARNED it is known that to gain wisdom it is sometimes necessary to hear like a child, see like a child, walk like a child and speak like a child. My son Ben, who as a nineteen year old still viewed life with a child's sense of wonder, illustrated the truth of these words when, for my sixty-fifth birthday, he gave me the following poem as his present.

HAPPY BIRTHDAY!
65ᵗʰ B-Day Poem

Well dad, you're sixty-five!
Sixty-five years of being alive.
Not a moment to waste, and look where you are,
A loving family, a great job, a beautiful wife, and 2 cars.
Sixty-five years of being alive.
Take a moment to think and came to realize you're
    healthy, you're happy, and you love what you do.

The doctor even told you that your body acts life it's 42.

You have offered and given, so now it is time to receive,

   take in all that you can, do not rush, just breathe.

Life is too precious to just throw away.

We should take in every moment as if it were our last day.

I now must thank you so deeply for giving me such a

   great life.

I feel incredibly blessed to be the son of you and your wife.

So there you have it, another poem from your son.

Happy 65th Birthday.

Now I'm gonna go play some drums.

With great love,

Ben

Parting Words

TO BE BORN and to die, unfoldings of the ultimate mystery of the universe, can be viewed, if our eyes are open wide and willing to gaze into the light in all of its depth, brightness and intensity, with a sense of wonder and awe. At those moments, we are moving in sync to the rhythm and call of the heavenly spheres as we embark upon journeys into the greatest of all divine mysteries and revelations—the cosmic cycle of birth and death, of death and birth, as self merges with timeless and endless universe.

It is fitting to conclude our journey into the realm of life's endings with an ode to the human possibility for experiencing life as an art form dedicated to living and dying well; to facing the demise of self with acceptance and serenity knowing that it will take both courage and fortitude to encounter life's endings. Yes, the web that connected us to those we love will be torn. Yet, rest assured, for in the darkness there are cosmic "spiders" at work spinning ties that bind us together beyond the limitations of space and time.

Living Life As A Stairway to Heaven

An excerpt from my journal.

I stare at the tabletop, the flowers in the bowl resting on its surface begin to glow iridescently. Shadows stir in the dark recesses of the room as if they were seeking form. My lover rises out of the lake, her right eye a rich yellow, her left eye a green emerald, and her third eye the color of blue sapphire. She opens her mouth to expose a ruby tongue and a cavern beckoning unto me to enter. I do so. A crystal clear stream flows before me, its banks luxuriant with a velvety cushion of clover and moss, so inviting I lie down on its softness and listen to the enchanting sounds of celestial harps.

She begins to dance, her turquoise necklace rubbing against her breasts make her nipples erect, their purple brown color in sharp contrast to her green eyes that were blue but a moment ago. Kissing me softly, I become lost in the golden luster of her love as I stand on the edge of a translucent and gleaming lake, my soul dwelling in a trance of ecstasy.

Memories of the year that has passed flood me. It has been a very good year. I journeyed with my son and daughter into manhood and womanhood as we traversed the realms of courage truth justice respect love compassion fulfillment and planetary consciousness and walked on the land and by the sea hand in hand with my wife as our honey dipped tongues uttered sweet words of love serving to remind us why we had joined together as husband and wife till not even death do us part and danced naked under the evening sky bodies sanctified and ecstafied by the experience of moonlight shining on two souls skin graced by the touch of leaves flowers and fruits of trees known as lemon lime orange avocado eucalyptus jackfruit Surinam cherry with eyes still saturated by the brilliant colors of a setting sun of a thousand years ago that still beautified the sky and with ears hearing songs of birds of both lesser and upper paradise and floated on blue ocean waters with no purpose in mind no place to go but to surrender to waves and currents flowing east to west and west to east learning once again to let go and blew kisses to stars in the night that dazzled the sky and set hearts ablaze and thrilled the soul and ignited imagination with visions of human possibility and marveled at rainbows traversing the sky east to west and north to south and cried as we wished good traveling to all those who have come and gone and all those who will come and go and all who asked how do you get to heaven and gazed upon the eternal residing in the crater of the house of the sun and sat under the shade of banana trees and listened with gratitude as they told of what it is like to keep on giving up your bananas in the name of service to humankind and renewed souls of our very own as we bore witness to the lovely and the beautiful and the eternal and ate flowers and flew away on the wings of wild passionate butterflies as the flame of my lover's kiss illuminated a thousand petaled lotus within me.

Epilogue

Thine own consciousness, shining, void, and inseparable from the Great Body of Radiance, hath no birth, nor death, and is the Immutable Boundless Light.

The Tibetan Book Of The Dead

DEATH IS COMING. Lord, have mercy on us.

Death does not come for us. We are life. We are death. Cry. Weep. Forgive. Ask for forgiveness. Give love. Receive love. Accept. Surrender.

Perhaps when we die, we will find ourselves standing in the presence of a god or goddess, however we imagine the divine one to be. Looking directly at the deity, we ask, "Is this heaven?" The divine one answers, "Heaven is this heaven? Why you just came from there."

Bless the world with the healing power of love. Hold your hands up and visualize the healing light of love streaming from your heart through your hands and out your fingertips as its blessing graces first your loved ones, and then expanding to bless the entire world. May all experience peace of mind, peace of body and peace of soul.

Let us look back on our lives and everything we have experienced during our lifetimes and realize we are still here. As long as we are alive, we have another chance at this thing called life, to make of life on earth a heaven. Is this not more than enough to give us hope and joy?

Acknowledgements

The author is grateful to the following for permission to use:

From *The Metta Institute* by Frank Ostaseski. *www.mettainstitute. org*.

From *Chrysalis End of Life Inspiration* by Loretta Downs. www. endoflifeinspiration.com.

From *Living Your Dying* by Stanley Keleman. Center Press, 1985.

From *The Ultimate Journey: Consciousness and The Mystery of Death* by Stanislav Grof. Multidisciplinary Association for Psychedelic Studies, 2006.

From *Psychedelic Drugs Reconsidered* by Lester Grinspoon and James Bakalar. The Lindesmith Center, 1997.

From, *The Living Goddess: Reclaiming the Tradition of the Mother of the Universe* by Linda Johnsen. Yes International Publishers, 1997.

From *Iwona's Story* by Iwona Biedermann. Personal Essay.

From *Barbara's Eulogy To Al* by Barbara Janoff Silverstein. Personal Essay.

From *I'm A Former Student Of Yours* by Chris . . . Personal Essay.

From *We All Have A Need* by Hazel Aura G.

From *Happy Birthday: 65th B-Day Poem* by Ben Cofresi-Silverstein.

About the Author

L OUIS SILVERSTEIN is a Professor of Liberal Education at Columbia College Chicago where he teaches courses in Peace Studies, Dying & Death, Education, Culture & Society, and Social Problems In American Society. His studies and presentations, theoretical and experiential, centered on transformative consciousness, alternative realities and the human journey have been of long duration, encompassing five decades—1960's to the present, and have taken him to settings throughout the U.S., and to Jamaica, Costa Rica, Canada and numerous European countries. He is married to Paula Cofresi-Silverstein, psychotherapist and artist, and is the father of a daughter, Ana Rebeca Cofresi-Silverstein, and a son, Ben Cofresi-Silvertstein.

Made in the USA
Monee, IL
26 June 2023

37618334R00114